EVERYONE IS AN AUTHOR

CONFESSIONS OF AN EXISTENTIAL AMATEUR

James R. Fisher, Jr., Ph.D.

Published in the United States of America

1. Psychology/Social & Cultural Psychology
2. Sociology/Cultural & Economic Anthropology
3. American Moral/Social Philosophy
4. Psychology/Industrial & Organizational Psychology 14.02.17
5. Published works with commentaries

For Henley James Fisher,

Our Great Grandson, born December 9, 2020

FOREWORD: EVERYONE'S AN AUTHOR

The seeds of this modest little book were planted a few years ago when I gave a talk at the Temple Terrace Public Library, Tampa, Florida, on May 20, 2014. Author Ernest Hemingway once said, *"There is nothing to writing. All you do is sit down at a typewriter and bleed."*

Hemingway, unable to be present to accept the Nobel Prize for Literature in Stockholm, December 10, 1954, due to ill health, had United States Ambassador, John Cabot read this acceptance speech:

"Having no facility for speech-making and no command of oratory nor any domination of rhetoric, I wish to thank the administrators of the generosity of Alfred Nobel for this Prize.

No writer who knows the great writers who did not receive the Prize can accept it other than with humility. There is no need to list these writers. Everyone here may make his own list according to his knowledge and his conscience.

It would be impossible for me to ask the Ambassador of my country to read a speech in which a writer said all of the things which are in his heart. Things may not be immediately discernible in what a man writes, and in this sometimes he is fortunate, but eventually, they are quite clear, and by these and the degree of alchemy that he possesses he will endure or be forgotten.

Writing, at its best, is a lonely life. Organizations for writers palliate the writer's loneliness but I doubt if they improve his writing. He grows in public stature as he sheds his loneliness and often his work deteriorates. For he does his work alone and if he is a good enough writer he must face eternity, or the lack of it, each day.

For a true writer, each book should be a new beginning where he tries again for something that is beyond attainment. He should always try for something that has never been done or that others have tried and failed. Then sometimes, with great luck, he will succeed.

How simple the writing of literature would be if it were only necessary to write in another way what has been well written. It is because we have had such great writers in the past that a writer is driven far out past where he can go, out to where no one can help him.

I have spoken too long for a writer. A writer should write what he has to say and not speak it. Again I thank you."

Phase One of being an author

Although we are all talkers, that we all have stories to tell, despite the delight we derive in sharing these stories, we still construct barriers that block us from ever starting to write them down.

But there is no barrier greater than "I can't do it. I can't write. I'm not smart enough to write." These barriers are clinchers. They stop us dead in the water.

I've never been the smartest kid on the block, but that has never been a barrier to me. I've never stopped to say, "I'm not qualified to write." It never occurred to me to be relevant.

One person who has known me all my life said, "I never thought you'd turn out this way."

"How is that, Gussie?"

"You know, as a writer, that kind of deep stuff."

What he didn't say but implied was, "Where'd you get the arrogance, Fisher, to think you could write?"

It wasn't arrogance. It was a need, a need to express myself in words, symbols, language to make a connection with my thoughts and feelings, beliefs and biases, loves and hates, dreams and fantasies, to make peace with my demons and dreads. Writing gave me a modicum of control.

The other thing is it made me feel comfortable in my own skin, comfortable with what I am and am not, can and can't do, where I need help (weakness) and what I do well (strength). *Writing introduced me to myself.* In other words, I've never let others define me.

Moreover, I've always been attracted to people smarter than I am, people from whom I could learn. This has included dead authors. My granddaughter, Rachel, is like her grandfather in that sense, and she is an outstanding student. I've been an outstanding student at every level of my education, receiving my share of academic honors despite an occasional misstep. I'm not saying you have to be a good student to be a writer. F. Scott Fitzgerald was a terrible student but a great writer, so was William Faulkner, and he won the Nobel Prize for Literature. With my insecurity, I needed the affirmation of academia.

I went from a Catholic grammar school to a public high school, and although an "A" student in the Catholic school, I was put in classes where "C" students were the norm. I suppose – in this Protestant community – a Catholic "A" was the equivalent of a Protestant "C."

Language was important in the Catholic school, especially grammar. My teacher in my freshman year of high school was struggling in diagramming a complex sentence before the class and became frustrated in the process. I went to the board, erased her work, and diagrammed the sentence properly, returned to my desk with a smile, and was promptly sent to the principal's office with a pink slip. It kept me out of the *National Honor Society*, although I graduated in the top 10 percent of my class, as I did at the *University of Iowa*, and in graduate school. I have received every academic honor offered at every grade level throughout my academic career with this high school exception because I paid attention albeit with periodic aberrant behavior that put my status in some jeopardy.

This is told to readers as I come from the lowest end of the food chain, and have known from the get-go that to climb up the ladder there would be no help, no safety net, no golden parachute, no convenient off-ramps to cool my jets, no one or nothing to break my fall. I was on my own nickel, and I was going to do it my way or it was for sure the highway.

To put it another way, if I can write books, anyone can write books. The only real qualification to write is to demonstrate the courage to start. You can't worry about what others think or whether you're qualified or not. No one owns that crystal ball.

Five things have worked for me as a writer: (1) I am not afraid not to be smart; (2) I'm not worried about letting the group down; (3) I'm not afraid of failure; (4) I accept the pain and the risk to coming up empty, which I often have; (5) when I succeed, and I have on occasion, I have no delusions of being other than the son of an Irish Roman Catholic brakeman on the railroad.

Readers of my books -- several people tonight have noted how wide and diverse my career -- try to define me, thinking

I am an extrovert. I am an introvert. People are my laboratory, and all my works emanate from that laboratory. I prefer only the company of my wife, Betty, and my books.

People wear me out. This (tonight) wears me out because I leave my energy behind when I leave.

Writing to me is serious business. It requires thinking, and thinking is like meditation, not something you do with others. We live in a society enamored of "groupthink," which I appall.

The satisfaction from writing comes in the doing, not in the concluding. We make too much of the product, not enough of the process. Stephen King has all the money he will ever need, but he is a compulsive writer, and admits it, once comparing it to trying to give up cigarettes.

So many books are written today because authors sense a connection with Aristotle's "rational man" in this most irrational of times. It has been my experience if you read for pleasure you will write for pleasure, too.

Phase Two of being an author

The newspaper lady in the back who is writing a book about the role God has played in her life can appreciate what my mentor told me about my audience, which is top management and professionals:

One is *"More is less."*

Two is *"You know that it* (could that be God?) *knows, and you know that it knows that you know, and you know that it knows that you know that it knows that you know."*

So, this limits gamesmanship. Neither the writer nor the reader can play dumb. This cuts to the quick. My mentor is wise and knows that I will struggle with this until it is my own.

Phase Three of being an author

Everyone has a story crying within to be told, and I suspect, that is the reason you are here.

How do you get started? How do you put yourself in the mood to begin?

Abraham Lincoln wrote and rewrote his *"Gettysburg Address"* while traveling to that destination, feeling he had failed, as he was not an orator. He spoke for a few minutes, while celebrated orator Edward Everett spoke for two hours.

Lincoln understood my mentor's admonition subconsciously if not consciously. Less proved more and Lincoln made the connection; Everett did not. Lincoln had a wheezing voice in his massive body, while Everett had a booming voice in his stout diminutive one.

Everett was a performer; Lincoln was a communicator. Lincoln was meditative, Everett was charismatic. Lincoln was an introvert; Everett an extrovert. Lincoln was writing to himself; Everett was speaking to an audience. Lincoln made a spiritual connection with himself and hit his target; Everett was a mechanic and spoke over their heads. Our times more resemble Everett than Lincoln. This should give us pause.

Someone asked: *"How do you get your thoughts and the way you speak to translate to make sense on the page?"*

Lincoln, who was essentially self-educated, an autodidact, read a lot, and loved the music of language, and came to master its rhythm and make it his own. For the rest of us, we have to simply practice, practice, and practice. Even then, it is difficult to match precisely what we think with what appears on the page.

My wife Betty chimed in, *"Jim talks to himself. He talks out loud as he thinks about what he is about to write."*

Yes, that is true. I must hear how it sounds *"out loud"* before I commit it to the screen. That said I write and rewrite and rewrite some more, as it takes several attempts before it makes sense to me, and resembles what I am thinking. Still, I am subject to many errors because I am an imperfect editor.

When I was back in my hometown researching my book on my youth (IN THE SHADOW OF THE COURTHOUSE), I would walk through the streets of this small town, tape recorder in hand, talking as I walked. Three African American boys stopped and stared at me.

One boy said, "Look at that man?"

The second boy said, "What?"

The third boy said, "Can't you see? He's talking to himself." He rolled his finger in a circle by his ear, "Crazy, man!"

"I'm talking into my recorder," I said. "I'm writing a book."

"Oh, yeah," they giggled in unison, "He's writing a book!"

Talking to myself is my way. It is not the only way, but it seems to help me match my thoughts with what eventually gets written. Now, it is hard to find cassettes for my micro recorder. Society has moved beyond my limited technology, but human behavior has not, which makes writing a constant as people throughout history remain essentially the same.

Phase Four of being an author

Genius is not rare, but pervasive. We often look for it in all the wrong places. That is also true in the case of writing. Genius has a conceptual foundation, not a recall foundation as displayed on such television game shows as "Jeopardy."

A few years ago, the *Temple Terrace Public Library* had a writing contest for young people nine to twelve to write what the library meant to them. Some forty young people participated. I had the privilege of being one of the reviewers.

Some of these essays were so pristine they looked as if they came out of a published book; some had a vocabulary that indicated more than a little help from a parent. Then there was one handwritten essay that stood above all the others.

It was captivating from the first sentence. For this writer, the library was a dream fulfilled. He said when I walk into the library -- and I'm paraphrasing now -- it opens up to me as if it belongs to me, and it directs me to where I want to go. I pick up a book, and my whole world changes.

I wrote in my evaluation that this essayist should one day be a writer. I wasn't there when they gave out the prize. Nor did I know that this writer had won. I understand that a little African American boy in the back of the room, rushed up to accept his prize grinning from ear to ear, saying to no one in particular, "Can you believe this!"

Phase Five of being an author

My daughter, Laurie, is a professional model. We share one common thread of professionalism, rejection! We are familiar with being rejected.

I came back from South Africa in 1969 something of a broken man after experiencing that assignment (see **DEVLIN – A Psychological Novel** – on Kindle), having retired (the first time) only in my thirties, writing to *The William Morris Agency in New York City* asking that agency to represent me as a writer. I had no idea how absurd that request was.

I told the agency that I *"had retired"* from my high-paying executive position to write books.

The William Morris Agency wrote me a blistering letter in reply, stating it thought it had heard everything, but that I took the cake, nothing was more maddening than what I had done or proposed to do. I still have the letter. I never heard from the agency again.

Hemingway advised a would-be-author to write about what he knew. I had written *"Sales Training & Technical Development"* in South Africa for the new company. So, when back in the States, I wrote a book on selling, which I completed in six weeks, and sent it off to *Prentice-Hall*, calling it *"Let's Take the Worry Out of Selling."* Two weeks later, it was accepted.

It was published with the title, **"Confident Selling,"** published in 1970 with a 1971 copyright.

The book sold 25,000 copies in the first two months, and was in print for 20 years, only with *Prentice-Hall's copyright*, not mine. Caution: *don't give up your copyright if you can help it.*

That was so easy that I sent other manuscripts off to a bevy of publishers receiving form rejection letters, enough to paper a room.

Discouraged, I turned my attention to reading books, then going back to school to earn my Ph.D., not publishing again until 1990 with **Work Withoug Managers** (1991).

At the same time, I launched a website with a blog, finding an open market for my essays in trade journals, newspapers, and periodicals. None of them paid me a sue. Only **Reader's Digest** did when I sent them *"Twenty Points of Light."* It was accepted in January 1993 with a check being received two weeks later for $2,000, saying the piece would be published

June 3, 1993. You have to sell a lot of books to make $2,000 in royalties.

The following month of that publication, **Reader's Digest** informed me in a letter that requests for reprints of that short article had passed 30,000. The first line of that piece: "To have a friend, you must be a friend, starting with yourself." This led to my writing of ***"The Taboo Against Being Your Own Best Friend"*** (1996).

Phase Six of being an author

If you think publishing a book is like winning the lottery, think again. If you want to be famous, want to be a celebrity, make a lot of money, read the blistering letter I received from the *William Morris Agency*.

There are hundreds of thousands of books published every year, especially in this era of *print-on-demand books* and *e-books* in which the authors don't make expenses. I'm one of such authors. I lost a bundle early in my writing career thinking everyone would want to read my works. Not true.

On the other hand, if you have the confidence, and have a passion to write if only your family reads your work, this could make it worthwhile. Remember, publishing is a business, and publishers have to find a lot of willing gamblers for them to afford to give large advances to celebrities whose book sales seldom match their advances.

A friend of mine is writing her family history. She is as genuine as they get. She was as a young girl, and now a grandmother with the same vigor and élan that she had as a youngster. She is writing her story, which should be appealing because she has lived a fascinating life.

My favorite cousin, who died a few years ago, wrote a book for his family titled *"An Insignificant Life."* I've never been able to read it because I become all choked up after the first few pages.

Robert earned a BSEE, went into the US Navy and became an officer in *Naval Intelligence*, and found himself in the Arctic at an outpost monitoring the Soviet Union's nuclear program. He was at his post in 1952 when Russia detonated its first hydrogen bomb, years ahead of what the CIA and NSA expected.

He alerted his commanding officer, who told him to call the White House, which he did with trepidation. Later, he went back to school and took a Ph.D. in economics, and became an economist for the State of Colorado. Insignificant my foot! But modesty was natural to him from his Norwegian side of the family.

Phase Seven of being an author

We desire to be authors because we want to make a connection, to get outside ourselves to connect with ourselves in another way. That is the mystique of the social network. How many here are on Facebook – most everyone. Do you feel connected? Of course, you do. We seek the approval of others to approve of ourselves.

It is too funny. We are not a reading public. Less than 10 percent of Americans are regular purchases of books, yet nearly everyone tweets, which requires reading. Put all the tweets together after a day, and it would likely make a fairly good-sized book. But it is not considered reading, certainly not book reading, so it is absolved from that connection. Who knows, maybe book reading one day will reach 11 percent.

The Information Age has made everyone readers despite themselves. I'm a fairly good typist. Now I learn typing is passé with all you need is two thumbs. Can you imagine that?

Phase Eight of being an author

I would encourage you to have a conversation with yourself, keep a diary, scribble notes, write poetry, or fragments of philosophy, as I did in the early 1970s. One day you will pick it up and say, "Wow!"

In my case, what I had written some thirty years ago seemed as relevant as if it had just been written. *"Time Out for Sanity! Blueprint for an Anxious Age"* was the title, which TATE Publishing will release later this year which was so generated. It occurred to me that my books are chapters of the same story:

- why do we remain stuck,
- why do we treat ourselves so poorly,
- why do we keep running from ourselves?

In the 1970s, the narcotic of our escape was psychedelic drugs, now it is the societal ubiquitous mobiles of social media. The irony is while we are prisoners 24/7 to our handheld electronic devices thinking we are networking with others we have little or no time to network with ourselves in wondering.

I am a confessed wonderer. That said, my books have no answers but attempt to ask the right questions. I believe that the problems we experience once honestly defined reveal the answers.

Twenty-four years ago *Work Without Managers* was thought to be angry, if not crazy, yet in 2014, it is clear we don't need managers. We don't need them at all, yet we still have them, and chances are 24 years hence we'll still have them. See why I think we are stuck? Our lies and deceits become our Tar Baby, and we get stuck on this barrier, ignoring the problems we face and solving the problems we don't face.

This is what I write about so I'm not surprised if I'm not a household name to you.   I'm encouraged, however, to hear from people like Eric, Klaus, and Ted who are in the audience. They stimulate my mind when they write, as they cut through all the folderol, and penetrate the nonsense.

Some of you may have your own strong views but are afraid to share them. You shouldn't. We are all trying to get inside the limits of language to the ideas buried inside.

My writing is meant to inspire people to have more confidence in themselves, and to take charge and control of their lives, as tenuous as that may be.

Our culture isn't serving us very well, yet it refuses to change. It is hard to get a sense of ourselves in a time of pervasive sameness. The lady writing about God in her life says she isn't religious but spiritual. Did we ever imagine a dichotomy between the two? It is hard to be spiritual in a secular world, and equally hard to be religious. That doesn't mean that we need to abandon the spiritual or religious but does mean we cannot count on others to carry our burdens, not politicians, pundits, priests, or prognosticators. I think that is wrong. That is why I write.© James R. Fisher, Jr., Ph.D., May 20, 2014.

THIS AUTHOR'S GENESIS

Many years ago, when I was quite young, and a professor at the University of Iowa, who was teaching one of the core courses in literature required for graduation, whatever your major, interviewed me for a midterm rather than have me submit a paper, as I had missed the class having been confined to the university's infirmary with infectious mononucleosis.

This condition would happen again as I would often study to the point of exhaustion with my immune system ultimately shutting down.

The subject of the midterm had been the works of Irish novelist, James Joyce (1882 – 1941), especially his biographical novel, *A Portrait of the Artist as a Young Man* (1916).

The professor commenced to ask me questions about the book, finding me provocatively interrupting him, and asking, *"Professor, could I tell you what I got out of this book?"*

Chain-smoking, he seemed relieved for me to do just that. Once I finished, a good hour later, covered in cigarette smoke, I studied his eyes through the haze, as he said, *"How do you come to understand Joyce so well?"*

I answered, matter-of-factly, *"I am Joyce."* The book dealt with Joyce's struggle with the Irish culture, the Catholic Church, especially the Catholic priesthood, and the seeming moral duplicity between what that the Catholic culture purported to be in contrast to what it was.

My professor looked at me for the longest time, and then said, *"What is your major?"*

"Chemistry."

"What are you doing in science?"

"I'm good at it."

"This is our first-ever conversation," he said more to himself than to me, *"and now I better understand your writing. You write broodingly personal unconsciously candid."*

"Kind alike Joyce's stream of conscious?" I offered to which he did not respond.

Lighting another cigarette on the one in his hand, he said, *"I'd like to recommend you for Iowa's Honors Program in the Humanities."* Stunned, I said nothing. *"Go home this weekend and discuss it with your parents, and get back to me next week,"* but as he was leaving, I asked, *"What exactly is the Honors Program in the Humanities?"*

"You'll read books in English literature and cultural history, write papers, attend seminars, and be doing essentially independent studies somewhat in the manner of Cambridge in Oxford, England."

My mother, who graduated from high school and read a book-a-day, mainly because she was hard-of-hearing, was receptive to the idea, whereas my da, a passenger brakeman on the Chicago & North Western Railroad, who ended his academic career after completing the seventh grade, said, *"What the hell is that?"*

I repeated what the professor had said and seen fire in his eyes. "I see that type on my trains, long hair, beards, reading weird books, hanging on each other, scruffy and smelling like they haven't bathed in a month." He lit a cigarette, took a long drag, and said, *"Jimmy, can I ask you a question?"* I nodded. *"You're not a goddamn fag are you?"*

I couldn't believe the question, and shouted, *"No!"*

Not apologizing for the question, he justified it by saying, *"I suspect these lazy bastards are."*

FIRST WATERSHED MOMENT

I stayed in chemistry and have had the career that I have had with this my **FIRST WATERSHED MOMENT** as writing, the pure act of putting down my thoughts as they occurred to me, was like taking an elixir. I was revitalized by the experience of finding writing an expression of thought which was clarified by seeing the words pour out of my soul.

Confident Selling (1971) would be written after returning from South Africa in 1969. It was an attempt to explain to myself why I had been so successful with Nalco Chemical Company over the previous decade, first as a chemical sales engineer, then field manager, and finally as an international executive.

A political operative read the manuscript that I completed in six weeks in 1970 and asked if he could send it to a publisher. He sent it to **Prentice-Hall, Inc., Englewood Cliffs, New Jersey.** Two weeks later the publisher sent a contract to me, which I signed without reviewing it, being surprised by the acceptance. The book would sell 25,000 copies the first month and be in print for 20 years with P-H holding the copyright. I would never again surrender my copyright to a publisher.

P-H did ask me to summarize the essence of **Confident Selling**, which would prove prophetic as it would represent my fundamental approach to dealing with people and organizations:

The key is the awareness and acceptance of yourself as you are, warts and all, which in turn enhances your inclination to accept others as they are and as they are found.

SECOND WATERSHED MOMENT

After a writing hiatus of 20 years (1970-1990), I would follow retire from Honeywell and devote my full time to writing, which represented a **SECOND WATERSHED MOMENT** in that I would write and publish **Work Without Manager: A View from the Trenches** (1991), which was a moral and structural assessment of the complex corporate organization. It would garner a lot of attention but quickly revealed that a writer who has little interest in the mechanization of publishing, needs an agent, which I did not have.

Work Without Managers tracked the chaotic consequences of the discernible shift from the position power of management to the knowledge power of professional workers without any discernible change in the distribution of power and control away from management and to this burgeoning workforce which had gone since WWII from 80 percent blue-collar to 80 percent white-collar and professional.

The collective denial of this dramatic shift in actual power has resulted in the creation of *Three Dominant Cultures*: *Comfort, Complacency, and Contribution*, with the emphasis on the first two.

[In June 1993, **The Reader's Digest** published one of my succinct articles, **"Do Unto Others"** in which the first sentence was, *"To have a friend, you must be a friend, starting with yourself."* R-D reported requests for copies were in the tens of thousands. Encouraged by this reception, **The Taboo Against Being Your Own Best Friend** (1996).]

The Reader's Digest, "Do Unto Others . . ."

James R. Fisher, Jr., June 1993

To have a friend, you must be a friend, starting with yourself.

The greatest hunger a person has is to be needed. Help create that feeling in others.

The greatest virtue is kindness. You can't love everyone, but you can be kind to everyone.

Don't try to impress others. Let them have the fun of impressing you.

Be enthusiastic. Nothing of consequence was ever achieved without enthusiasm.

Be positive. Positive people attract others, while negative people repel.

Gossip cheapens the one who gossips more than the one gossiped about.

Call a person by his or her name and use it often in conversation.

Communicate cheerfully.

Differences are bound to occur and can be resolved if the conflict is managed politely.

If you are given to making fun of someone, be sure it is of yourself.

Be genuinely interested in others. Get them to talk about themselves.

A smile doesn't cost anything and pays big dividends. Not only does it make you feel good, but it makes everyone else feel better too.

Be the first to say, "Hello! Good to see you.

Do unto others as you would have them do unto you."

The golden rule is where it all begins and ends.

In 1995, a slender volume, The Worker, Alone! Going Against the Grain was published to encourage professionals to take charge, and to do so by being responsive, responsible, and accountable for the success of the organization. A quarter-century later, 2020, there is little evidence that professionals have taken up this challenge.   I write:

The Worker, Alone claims professionals have no choice but TO GO AGAINST THE GRAIN for nothing changes until they do. The game of charades with empowerment continues because it is safe. It changes nothing and costs those in power even less. The costs are absorbed by the workers. Not until The Worker Alone realizes it is up to him to put his house in order, will change occur. Ventilation won't do it, nor will pointing fingers. The worker must "get off the dime" and take charge of work, which is the only way for him to take charge of his life

Professionals, as if still blue-collar workers, were programmed before WWII to be passive and reactive rather than active confronting management with this power disparity between management and workers, resulting in professionals retreating into Six Silent Passive Behaviors – *Passive Aggression, Passive Responsive, Passive Defensive, Approach Avoidance, Obsessive-Compulsive* and *Malicious Obedience behaviors*. Behaving as if "social termites," these silent behaviors were unlikely to be discovered until it was too late for damage control.

The CEO of *St. Lucie Press*, Florida contacted me in 1997 and said he would like me to expand on my thesis of the burgeoning professional and the "six silent killers" in a new book. With a contract in hand, I wrote the book, Six Silent Killers: Management's Greatest Challenge (1998). Unfortunately, the CEO died of a heart attack before the book was published, and *CRC Press* took ownership of the publisher.

CRC Press wanted to avoid publishing this book, claiming the publisher was going in a different direction. I had a contract, and I made them stick to it, attaining a lawyer to assure that certainty. Reviewers had much praise for this book, including *The Wall Street*

Journal, but *CRC Press* failed to promote the book, and so it died on the vine.

THIRD WATERSHED MOMENT

A **THIRD WATERSHED MOMENT** was in its nascent stage when I read Garry Wills' **"Papal Sin: Structure of Deceit"** (2000) where he documents the papacy's steadfast refusal to face the truth about itself, its past, and its relation with others. I immediately started to write about **"Corporate Sin"** (September 2000), which was apparent in my previous works, but the focus now was more specifically on **"Leaderless Leaders and Dissonant Workers,"** in the context of the subtle but unacknowledged paradigm shift from muscular masculine management to the less obstreperous and self-conscious feminine paradigm.

Actually, since 1993 with the success of **The Reader's Digest** article, I commenced exploring the possibility of writing a memoir as a novel about growing up as a preteenager in the middle of the United States, in the middle of the century, and the middle of a community, on the eastern crescent of the State of Iowa of the Mississippi River.

Over ten years (1993 – 2003), I would return to my hometown of Clinton, Iowa nearly a score of times traveling from my home in Tampa, Florida, a distance of nearly 1300 miles, to interview more than 100 Clintonians who were young in the middle of the 20th century. I also spent hundreds of hours viewing the microfiche records of **The Clinton Herald**, reading everything I could find on Clinton, including the book, **History of Clinton County Iowa**, published in **Clinton, Iowa's Bicentennial Year** (1976) by **The Clinton County Historical Society** (CCHS), an organization with which I have spent countless hours going through its archives and have been a patron ever since.

The seemingly pervasive cyclic nature of society, even in the short term, caused me to reflect on producing **"A Look Back to See Ahead"** (2007). We seem to survive the terrible '60s' only to drop precipitously into the frightening '70.' I write:

"The early 21st century is not like unlike the 1970s when young people were forced to participate in an unpopular war (Vietnam War); when political upheaval was in the air; when corrupt politicians who lied and deceased the electorate reached a crescendo with Watergate; when drugs were ruining lives; when morality took a holiday; when new forms of bigotry and hatred were hatching; when the automotive industry was in sharp decline, while foreign automakers were eating our lunch; when an energy crisis rocked the land with OPEC's oil embargo; when a paranoid president hunkered down and became a law unto himself; when Congress stayed the same, missed the changes, wouldn't face them, and left the future up for grabs. Sound familiar?

Well, it should because today we are stuck in the 1970s, and haven't found a way to be unstuck. "A Look Back to See Ahead" cuts through the psychobabble to show that talent is not enough to find happiness; nor is a winning personality with its many masks enough to ensure success. Each of us must find emotional balance in an irrational world because the heart can get us into a lot more trouble than the head. We must break through our cool façade, canned rhetoric, and mania for being insiders recognizing the "wisdom of insecurity" to move from nonsense to sense, shattering the "big lie" that science holds the key to our wellness as it is not immune to the same disease. Only we can unlock that door with this an invitation to do just that.

Between 2007 and 2012, I published no books but continued a vigorous publishing schedule writing scores of journal articles for such publications as National Productivity Review, The Journal of Organizational Excellence, The Journal of Quality & Participation, Executive Excellence, Personal Excellence, Sales & Marketing Excellence, The Conference Board of Canada, among others, while speaking at conferences in Toronto, Canada, Chicago, New Orleans, and Miami. Many of these articles presented at these conferences or penned for these publications would eventually become books.

FOURTH WATERSHED MOMENT

While surely seeming to be melodramatic, my life change in late December 2012 when Tate Publishing Company of Mustang,

Oklahoma offered me a contract to publish nine of my books as second editions and one book as a first edition. It proved a mix-blessing and therefore a FOURTH WATERSHED MOMENT.

Tate Publishing normally asked for the author's financial participation in the process. When I indicated I was not interested in making such an investment, they demurred saying they would make an exception in my case.

At the same time, Chris Carlin, Director of WWW.AMAZON.COM KINDLE print and e-book program, contacted me stating that Amazon wanted to publish "all my books" in this new medium, as well as any novels I had written.

In one sense, I was ecstatic but in another sense crestfallen as not being very competent on the Internet, and having all of my manuscripts, published and unpublished, in my Microsoft Drive, one day, accidentally, I had hit the wrong button and erased all my files. I had been told that nothing is "lost in the cloud," so I hired a computer engineer to retrieve these files, but alas, he was unable to do so.

Chris Carlin said, "No problem!" He asked if I had copies of all my books. I said I did. "Send us the books and we will turn them into computer files," which he did.

Tate Publishing, for my books to be second editions, wanted them to be (1) updated; (2) edited; (3) expanded; (4) made architecturally professional and user friendly.

This would necessitate essentially rewriting all of these books with constant submission and rejections until the books were considered publishable. What made this a "Watershed Moment" is that it resulted in changing my daily routine.

Normally, I would write for no more than three hours, read for a similar amount of time, and walk three miles every day through the Temple Terrace neighborhood. From January 2013 through December 2017, I would write for six to eight hours without a break, take a two-hour nap, and return to check and correct what I had written that day for about two hours. I no longer walked at all and suffered a severe infection in the groin area as I no longer showered every day. My son-in-law David Ewing recommended an ointment for my groin that eventually proved successful along with returning to my routine of daily showers.

During this four-year ordeal, my Beautiful Betty constantly reminded me that my new routine was ruining my health and that the effort was not worth the sacrifice. She had never ill-advised me but, sadly, I did not heed her, as this is what I always wanted – to have my ideas out there for others to consider – and I was now in the autumn of my years and still had my energy and passion to produce with my mind as supple, in my estimation, as it had been years earlier.

My suspicion that there are tens of thousands of amateur writers who have put off following their passions until they could afford it, not wanting to go through the desperate period of poverty and rejection that a James Joyce or a Samuel Beckett endured, indeed, as a Kurt Vonnegut, Jr. experienced, and thousands if not millions of others.

In 1969, even though I had a wife and four young children to support and a very promising career, I left Nalco Chemical Company and took a two-year sabbatical to read, think and write, moving from South Africa to South Western Florida in Clearwater. *Confident Selling* was written in six weeks, sent off to *Prentice-Hall, Inc.* without preamble or agent, and was accepted two weeks later, and published in September 1970 with a 1971 copyright.

It was not an author-friendly contract, and I signed away my copyright to P-H, which became an unwise decision on my part through ignorance of the publishing industry. *Confident Selling* became a national bestseller with an hour-long personal interview on *PBS television* with a television consortium coming to me with an interest in promoting the book with an audiotape and televised production. That opportunity went nowhere when it was clear I did not have the copyright authority for such exposure.

P-H had the book in production for twenty years or until 1991 when the publisher signed copyright authority over to me. *Top of the Mountain Publishing* with a staff of editors, artists, and marketers, next came to me wanting to publish an expanded version of Confident Selling with the title, *"Confident Selling for the 90s,"* publishing the book with me maintaining copyright authority in 1992.

TATE PUBLISHING'S NEFARIOUS FATE

The publishing industry in the 21st century is changing radically while not changing at all. Traditional publishers are still turning out instant reads and appealing polemics to meet the fickle tastes of readers in this Internet electronic age. TATE PUBLISHING, in an otherwise normal period, might have survived intact, but this is not a normal period.

Jeff Bezos' Amazon.com Kindle Library is publishing over one million books of writers without agents or portfolios and making billions for the exercise. Meanwhile, TATE, near bankruptcy and being forced to entertain nefarious pursuits, pleaded no contest to 44 criminal charges including embezzlement, attempted extortion, conspiracy, and racketeering in December 2019. Many authors invested with the publisher. The Canadian County, Oklahoma district court has issued an order that TATE will reimburse these customers some $900,000 for their losses over the next 20 years. Since I made no financial investment, I was not a party to these proceedings.

However, the tens of thousands of hours I spent recreating these second editions are my folly in one sense and my entertainment in another sense. Since I hold the copyright to all ten of these books with one first edition, many have been published by my own publishing company, The Delta Group Florida on Kindle, both in print and as e-books. A brief review of these ten books follows.

Confident Selling, 2nd Edition (2014) – Originally published in 1971

The premise of CONFIDENT SELLING is that you are the world, and if you know how to look and learn, then the door is there, and the key is in your hand. Nobody can give you that key, or open that door but you. Another premise is that we are all selling something. Therefore, we are all sellers. If selling is your profession, and you have what it takes, but haven't reached your true potential, then this book is for you.

CONFIDENT
SELLING
SECOND EDITION
Dr. James R. Fisher, Jr.

Confident Selling was about the seller being a learner of the buyer's needs rather than a teller of what he should do and a listener rather than a teller. A buyer most likely has similar problems to the seller's customers. Allow him to tell you about his operations.

Having been a chemist and familiar with flow diagrams, I would get behind the desk with the buyer and draw a schematic of his operation as he explained it to me, labeling areas in which I had experienced problems, asking if that was true of him. In that manner, without first realizing it, I was acting as a partner or extension of his staff.

At the time, a book titled "Winning through Intimidation" was a national bestseller. *Confident Selling* was the antithesis of this approach. I would return to university in 1970, becoming a full-time student for six years, consulting on the side, with my focus now on the soft rather than the hard sciences, necessitating taking many undergraduate courses first in the new discipline in quest of a Ph.D. is social, industrial, organizational psychology.

Once a Ph.D. was earned, in 1980 I joined Honeywell Avionics in Clearwater, Florida as a management and organizational development psychologist and subsequently as Director of Human Resources, Planning & Development in Brussels, Belgium with Honeywell Europe, SA.

From the pages of the 2nd edition of Confident Selling (2014)

This book is written for anyone who has reached an emotional or intellectual crisis that *confidence* can resolve. Such a person may be flustered by a loved one, a peer, a boss, or a business associate; by work, school, or life in general. The result is always the same — unnecessary worry and frustration, leading to sluggishness and ultimately, to *psychological inertia.* This book will help you through the adjustment period until you are confidently hitting on all cylinders.

DEALING WITH *FORWARD INERTIA*

This psychological inertia might be called *forward inertia.* It is like having your foot on the accelerator and brake at the same time, burning up rubber but going nowhere. The result of this inertia is the condition called "burnout," or in extreme cases, "a nervous breakdown."

Typically, the person with forwarding inertia is farther behind at the end of the day than when they started. They love their work but hate their job. Increasingly, they wonder, "Why bother? Who cares, anyway?" Chucking it all becomes more than a passing fancy. They feel hostage to career, work, home, and life in general, captive to an existence they hate, but powerless to change their circumstances.

Such a person ends up having little confidence in themselves and even less in others. With no hope for a more promising future, they become whimpering robots, feeling isolated and miserable. They begin to suffer from cynicism, pessimism, self-doubt, suspicion and end up with a case of arrested development. Eventually, they screw themselves into the ground and let the rest of the world go on without them.

This book can help reverse this crippling process by easing your foot on the brake and giving you the poise to adjust acceleration to take you where you want to go.

No Matter What You Do, This Book Is for You!

"Everyone lives by selling something."

Robert Louis Stevenson (1850-1894), author of *"Treasure Island"*

You are the possessor of a legacy, and that legacy is selling. *Salesmanship* is essential to our character. Why something so central to our lives and happiness should be marginal to what we treasure is a cultural oddity. Selling is the noblest and human of all civilized activities.

Look to the greatest statesmen in government, religion, industry, commerce, education, and the military and, without exception, what is pivotal to their success is the ability to win followers to their cause.

Those who have embraced selling as a professional career are among the chosen. But this book is not written only for them, but for everyone because, we all live by selling something – a product, a service, an idea, and always. . . ourselves.

What separates us from being successful at selling is a single factor, *confidence.* With confidence, the natural flow of awareness, acceptance, and appropriate action rush to our aid with miraculous speed. Before this can occur, however, real and imagined barriers must be removed. Nothing worthwhile is ever easy. Growth, which is another word for success, involves pain and risk. If it didn't, many more would be confident; many more would have achieved emotional and economic security.

Remember, success is never an end, but an exciting and continuous journey in which pain and passion are part of our common baggage.

Expect there will be highs and lows, good days and bad days, surprises and disappointments, tragedies and comedies, unions and separations.

When one realizes this is all part of the landscape of confidence, *awareness, acceptance,* and *action* take on new meaning:

- *Awareness* of the needs of others with whom we are dealing;
- *Acceptance* of things as they are (values, beliefs, interests, and expectations of others);
- *Acting* on this empowering knowledge in user-friendly terms to the mutual benefit of all concerned.

A CRISIS IN CONFIDENCE

A crisis in confidence is apparent. "Rant and rave" journalism has chronicled this crisis, finding it in all aspects of our society.

Confidence is what makes human beings human. One does not have to look too far to see this declining. Confidence fuels trust which supports cooperation, collaboration, and communication. Distrust kindles conflict, competition, and character assassination, dissipating precious energy. This throws us off stride until finally, in frustration, we lose our concentration and then our will to prevail.

This is not a book for the person who is looking for a *get rich quick* scheme, or for the miracle solution to a personal dilemma. While we may verbalize it otherwise, the purpose of our life is what we do. Life is not about thinking but doing. It is not about justifying what hasn't been accomplished or possessed, but what has been experienced spiritually and intellectually as well as materially.

What we do defines us and tells us who and what we are if we will but look and listen to the rhythm of our own lives. We are the person we expect to be and we develop the experiences and relationships we think we deserve. Beyond that, we have as much success and happiness as we can embrace our resistance to experiencing that success and happiness. Having a brain and a mind allows us the magnitude of such options, as intelligence is not an arbitrary I.Q. index; intelligence is what it does.

This book is therefore written for those who are close to *turning things around* but cannot seem to *make it happen.* The love relationship remains fragile; a peer will not let up from giving them a hard time; the boss continues to harass them, failing to appreciate their value; hot prospects remain frustratingly just that – *hot prospects.* The big break they've been waiting for continues to escape them, even though they can feel it in their bones. It is also written for those who find themselves invariably defensive, making excuses to every insight – their family, friends, and employers for not realizing the success that everyone expected of them. Yes, it is written for those who find themselves blaming loved ones, bosses, colleagues, customers, and prospects; their priests, ministers or rabbis; even their jobs and companies – everyone and everything but themselves for their failure to make satisfactory progress in life, all for the lack of confidence.

Work Without Managers: A View from the Trenches, 2nd Edition (2014) – Originally published in 1991

Work Without Managers offers an in-depth, systematic analysis of why the health of the American organization has suffered since the end of WWII. More than merely another treatise on quality and productivity, it cuts to the core of current corporate illness, management's refusal to face and deal with the continuing power shift from managers to professional workers. Topic prudent to this study: who holds the key to America's economic future; how has corporate culture come to inadvertently spawn "six silent organizational killers"; what is the corporation doing to make it gender-neutral in hiring, promoting, paying, and developing; what is the dominant corporate culture, where do you find it, how do you identify it; how do you bridge the growing corporate gap competence and cooperation; what does the complex organization need to do now not only to survive but prevail?

DR. JAMES R. FISHER, JR.
WORK
SECOND EDITION
WITHOUT
MANAGERS
A VIEW FROM THE TRENCHES

From 2nd edition of Work Without Managers (2014)

Managers! Who Needs Them?

Likely it seems far-fetched at first glance, a workplace absent of managers. After all, who among us has experienced a workplace without this all-important class of working professionals? And they seem to be multiplying, not diminishing in numbers. Everyone wants to be a manager, and the B-Schools are flourishing. We're sold on management. Yet, the more management is emphasized and the more we have managers, the less successful and fulfilled we seem to be as individuals and as a society. Ominously, our institutions and corporations are continuously teetering on the brink of ruin.

Something doesn't add up. Could it be that management as a field is not the panacea we have been led to believe? Perhaps managers do not have the answers we all thought they did.

Why Work Is Not Working Like It Ought To

We've all experienced it. Our employers seem to expect something quite different from us than what we expect of ourselves; that we know we are capable of doing. Their expectations of us are quite low in terms of our standards of behavior and the quality of our work.

Our performance is constantly judged, micro-measured in fact, but what is judged and measured seems to have little to do with what we feel ought to be important to an employer. While we may have as much or more education and experience than managers above us do, we are treated like school kids. And therein lays the problem.

We are no longer dependent on adults as we once were for guidance, discipline, and ideas. We are adults. We like our work and we're full of ideas and energy. We are ready to be tapped, to be activated, but with trust and acceptance.

Managers do not know this; do not understand the huge potential sitting right under their noses. How do we tell them? Well, we don't because we think they should already know this. We're the audience. Remember, that is our dutiful programmed role. And we have passively accepted this role for a long time; too long. In fairness, the threat of termination, rarely stated, is always inferred in every exchange between managers and the managed. Speaking up is death, as it were. Call it bullying if you wish.

Further, the environments, organizations, and cultures in which we work are hard to fathom. They seem designed to be ineffective. We're told our job is one thing, but the culture and the organization seem to conspire against our doing the job properly. Our work is simply not very important to the managers we needed to be supporting us. They seem too busy to even notice us at times. Yet, we know our work is important; they told us it was. When we inform our managers about these inconsistencies, they accuse us of being the problem. We shut up. The organization continues chaotically along, while conflict and political maneuvering steadily siphon vital energy out of the enterprise and us.

So, let's consider what we have. By actions, if not by intentions, we have a highly trained and motivated workforce of professionals who are assumed by management to be unmotivated, undisciplined, and unintelligent with managers who believe their job is to retrain, redirect, correct, manipulate and motivate these professionals, when these knowledge workers know as much or more about the postmodern business climate and its demands, than management.

To compound the problem, the workplace environment is structured, unintentionally we must suppose, to frustrate the efforts of professional workers to create and deliver their work. As problems arise, they are dealt with as localized disturbances or dismissed as the misunderstandings of simple-minded workers. What could be more absurd?

To state this unequivocally, I am serious about a workplace without managers. We need not be constrained by the past, as we now are. We are free to discard our outdated and unexamined assumptions about work, workers, and workplaces. And, most excitingly, we're ready to harness the vast dormant potential embodied by the best educated, most well-intentioned, and informed workforce that has ever existed. At the same time, we'll be releasing the potential of our companies and institutions to excel in their own right to serve the common good.

The Bigger Picture

We have been flummoxed. The present became the future, without warning. A spate of books, not long ago, sought to ease our discomfort by 'explaining away' the apparent contradictions. We've read Alvin Toffler's *"Future Shock"* and Dennis Gabor's *"Inventing a Future"* and Barbara Ward's *"Lopsided World,"* as well as C. P.

Snow's *"Two Cultures."* They were all reasonable books but changed nothing.

To be fair, these books thoroughly described the fundamental dislocations of society and the broad trends. What they failed to do was explain why and thereby increase our understanding of where we were going, how we'd get there, and why we ought to be going in that direction.

Work Without Managers: A View from the Trenches published more recently, attempted to answer these important questions. Some reviewers found the book "angry" others reacted favorably. These were respected publications, like *Industry Week* (named *WWMs* one of the ten best business books of 1991), *The Business Book Review-Journal* (one of the four major works of 1991 in its category), and NPR radio's *All Things Considered* said:

This is not casual corporate bashing; Work Without Managers is premeditated capital punishment of standard managerial systems that Fisher thinks have outlived their prime and may not have been useful even then.

Tellingly, it touched a nerve in certain quarters. That nerve has spread as if the organization had the shingles. Among other things, Work Without Managers argued that the First Industrial Revolution was over in 1945:

"A shocking look at American business; <u>why</u> it operates in '1945 nostalgia,' as Six Silent Killers threaten to destroy it; and <u>how</u> only American Leadership can still save the day!"

About the same time this was being published, control theorist Russell L. Ackoff proposed that the world was going through a Second Industrial Revolution. He wrote:

"Since World War II, we have entered into a period, which will be to the future what the Renaissance was to the past. We have moved into a new age that is fundamentally different from the age, which we have

*come, an age that began with the Renaissance and ended essentially
with World War II."*

Ackoff's ideas align with sociologist Pitirim Sorokin's hypothesis. He
published *Social and Cultural Dynamics* (1937), scores of years before
the Ackoff thesis. Sorokin postulated the theory that we were at the end
of a 600-year *"Sensate Day."* His *"Sensate Day"* commenced with the
high Renaissance of 1500 A.D. in Italy, and ended with the First
Industrial Revolution. Thus, we are living in Ackoff's Second Industrial
Revolution, and are entering Sorokin's 600-year *"Ideational Day"* of
the glorious tomorrow.

Remarkably, two theorists, generations apart, envisioned the same
phenomenon, the end of one historic era and the dawn of another,
differing only in their descriptive nomenclature.

The Paradox

We have departed the Old Machine Age and have entered the New
Machine Age, characterized by microprocessors, satellites, software,
robotics, and cyberspace. You may know it as the Information Age.
Regardless, it's all very new and exciting, liberating in fact. Yet this
New Machine Age is encumbered with some troublesome remnants of
the past, principally a devotion to *reductionism.*

Reductionism is a method that seeks to reduce complex systems, to
collections of parts, to understand and manage them efficiently. Each
part is then small enough to be understood and managed independently.
The disciples of reductionism, who are legion, fervently believe it to be
the only way to understand and manage complex systems. For the most
part, no one even questions this methodology. In truth, it is not often
spoken of as reductionism. It's taken for granted and mostly goes
unrecognized.

Ironically, reductionism is so ubiquitous in the computer age. As a
method of analysis and control, it has been popular for well over a
century, applied in virtually every field: atoms in physics, cells in
biology, indices in economics, and Freudian elements of personality

(id, ego, and superego) or Skinner's conditional stimulus and response behaviorism in psychology.

Societal Reflex Thinking

Although some disciplines have moved away from reductionism, our cultural reflex is still to default to reductionism. It is evident in our susceptibility to simplistic solutions, particularly to stubborn complex problems. It is also the strongest indication that management, in general, is "out of sync" with the workplace of our times. Management loves simplifications; it runs from complexity, while it vociferously denies this practice.

Although narrow logic dominated Machine Age Thinking, and the limits of linear logic in this non-linear age are increasingly apparent, these limits have not been sufficient to discourage their dominance. Like the limits of linear logic in this non-linear age, causation has not always proven reliable.

During the First Machine Age, the concept of environmental stewardship was unimaginable. People lived in "closed systems" obedient and unquestioning of dogmas that drove the workings of industrial society; a world of discrete parts with no explanation provided to workers about how they all worked together.

People came to understand and to be constrained by the notion that the whole could never be greater than the sum of its parts. Today, we know that is not true, but oddly, we do not usually act on that knowledge.

Mistaken Certainties

Machine Age thinking also relied on a process called "analysis," which was similarly governed by reductionism. To explain something, such as the workings of a large organization, it was first reduced to its elemental parts, figuratively and actually. These parts were analyzed, optimized, and then given their own goals. Consistent with the linear logic of Socratic thinking, these components were explained in the context of a particular problem. Management called it "cutting the problem down to size." Meanwhile, in the world of psychology, the structure of behavior was reduced to the phenomena of discrete syndromes.

Realistically, most problems don't respond to this breakdown because it is not meant to deal with complexity, myriad interactions of parts and people. The result is that the problems solved are generally not the problems faced. "Paralysis by Analysis" is the term given to this absurd occurrence, where the original problem is forgotten in the process. We still do this, more often than not.

HR Reductionism

Reductionism in the office, among professional knowledge workers, has been a disaster. How can you break down knowledge work into independent specialized functions and then reassemble the work performed, expecting reasonable "results"? Incredibly, managers believe it can be done. On paper, the *expected* vs. *achieved results* appear to correlate, but in reality, there is only too frequently a large gap.

Consider the Machine Age concept of "Management by Objectives" (MBOs) championed by Peter Drucker, a master of reductionism. He introduced MBOs as a rationally ordered way to achieve corporate goals. His intentions were good, but the concept was not. Widely adopted by corporations, it soon became, simply, a ritualistic exercise, eventually fading away.

This has happened with numerous, rational sounding, corporate management theories, appropriate for factory-like operations, treating people as products with standardized expectations. For instance, the infamous *Performance Appraisal System* (PAS) was meant to be a coaching, counseling, guiding, and directing mechanism to improve workers' performance. Instead, it reinforced management chain-of-command control of professionals who were confined to a labyrinth of cubicles, while managers dispensed modest pay increases and, for the effort, stifled professional development.

From the mid-twentieth century on, fad theories continued percolating as to how to assess this changing workforce and gauge their problem-solving contributions. These fads included the value of symbols, charismatic management, cosmetic interventions, communication schemes, leadership style paradigms, and finally, engineering cybernetics.

That is, the workplace was recognized as a "system" consistent with control theory, which provided a template for evaluating and accepting or rejecting these previous theories.

Unconscious Incompetence

Today, unconsciously, most organizations, de facto, are still committed to Machine Age thinking, and reductionism, but ironically, in a rather more vigorous way.

These organizations, private and public, for-profit and non-profit practice reductionism by reducing the system to discrete autonomous elements: that is, departments, divisions, functions, and technologies. Ackoff cautions this is a self-defeating strategy if this is not understood:

The performance as a whole is affected by every one of its parts. That is a basic characteristic of a system. If you think of a corporation as a system, this means that every department (division, technology, function) can affect the performance of the corporation. That is the first condition of a system. If you have a department, which does not affect the performance of the corporation, the one thing you can be sure of is that it is not a part of the corporation.

The second characteristic of a system is that the way that any part affects the whole depends on what one other part is doing. No part of the system has an independent effect on the whole. What this says is that the way marketing affects corporate behavior depends on what other departments do, and vice versa.

Now the third condition is the most complex. If you take these elements (components) and group them in any way, they form subgroups. These subgroups will be subject to the same first and second conditions as the original elements were, that is, each subgroup will affect the performance as a whole and no subgroup will have an independent effect on the performance of the whole.

Ackoff argues this is the difference between an indivisible part and an indivisible whole in which the roots of the current Intellectual Revolution lay.

Standing Back

Systems Thinking is the new approach to problem-solving and organizational effectiveness. It means moving from a preoccupation with parts to a new concentration on the whole of things, the wholes of which they are apart. This is a shift from analysis to synthesis.

With analysis, if you wanted to explain a problem, you took it apart, explained the parts, then put it back together again, explaining the problem in terms of the parts.

In synthesis, if you wanted to explain a problem, you did exactly the opposite. You didn't look at the problem to be explained as a whole to be taken apart but as a part of a greater whole. You explain the whole of which it is a part and then extract an explanation of the thing you started with from an explanation of the whole.

If this sounds confusing, it is because of our conditioning. It may seem to be counterintuitive thinking, which often comes into play in OD work. Ackoff comes to our aid:

If you consider a system and take it apart to identify its components, and then operate those components in such a way that every component behaves as well as it possibly can, there is one thing of which you can be sure. The system as a whole will not behave as well as it can. The corollary is this, if you have a system that is behaving as well as it can, none of its parts will be.

Consider some advantages to counterintuitive thinking:

It nullifies the practice of interdepartmental competition and validates the synergistic power of cooperation.

It abhors the idea of comparing and competing in a drive to excellence as it cheapens a central focus and instead becomes a second-hand imitation of an excellent company as a model. Unequivocally, with a central focus, people in the company realize they are sitting on acres of diamonds.

It acknowledges the workplace isn't working like it used to work. Counterintuitive thinking may not have been critical to Machine Age thinking but is essential to *Systems Thinking*.

The Cure is Known

Ackoff's theorem, as you see, has special significance to *Work Without Managers*. In my more than forty years working in corporations at every level of organization on four continents, I have found the absence of control theory to be of devastating consequences. In this original work (1991) I wrote:

Take Corporate America. Any large company today is 20 to 30 divisions in search of a corporation. The pendulum of centralization-decentralization is more a yo-yo contest with no clear winners, only painfully confused losers. Trauma is written on the face of American enterprise. Meanwhile, this once powerful and energetic nation doesn't seem to know what is happening.

I wish it were possible to declare that Corporate America has changed, but as you read this book, you will see it has changed little. While work has evolved from brawn power to brainpower, from blue to white-collar, from managers to professionals, from assembly lines to software manufactured products, from brick, mortar and steel institutions to online universities at a fraction of the cost of higher education, from distinctive technological disciplines to complex hybrids, and from hierarchies and position power to Skunk Works and knowledge power, managerial approaches have not changed.

The failure to embrace *System Theory* continues to throw Corporate America off its stride, and thus every worker. Think of how you can apply the lessons learned here to your job, and by extension to operations in general. The first step is to take charge of your work, which is the best way to take charge of your life. Damn the torpedoes. We don't need managers. They need us.

ASCENT
OF THE
WORKING
WOMAN

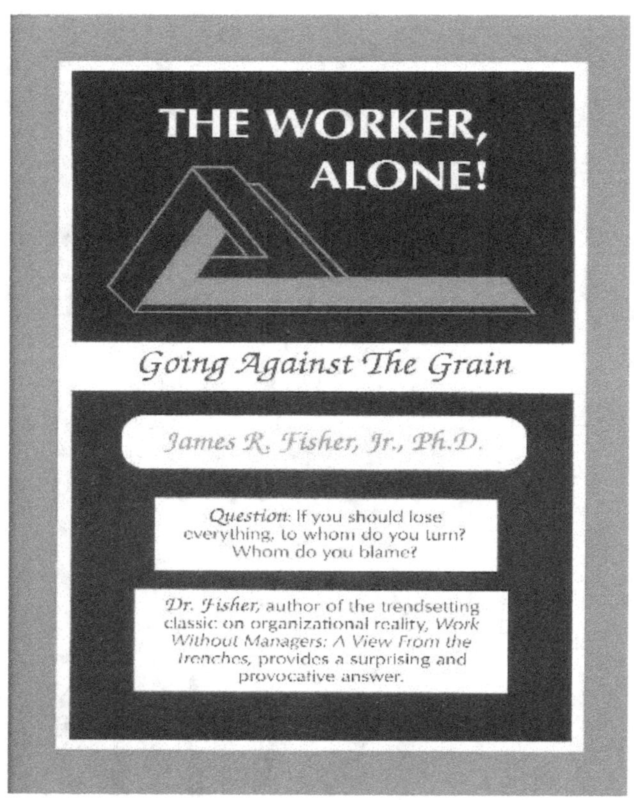

From the 2nd edition of ASCENT OF THE WORKING WOMAN (2017)

THE UNITED STATES OF ANXIETY

No Longer a "Glass Ceiling," now simply a WALL buried in Gender Statistics

Some twenty-two years ago, viewing women through the *feminine prism* in an attempt to get inside the gender bias, a chapter of *The Taboo against Being Your Own Best Friend* (1996) was dedicated to male/female statistics:

In 1996, white boys got higher scores in mathematics and science, while girls got higher scores in reading, writing, and reading comprehension;

Boys in eighth grade were 50 percent more likely to be held back a grade than girls; boys in high school constituted 68 percent of the special education population;

67 percent of female high school graduates went on to college, whereas 58 percent of male high school graduates did so.

Regarding graduate school in 1970:

Women received 40 percent of all master's degrees and were 59 percent of all master's degree students in 1996, earning 53 percent of all master's degrees;

Women earned only 6 percent of all professional degrees (medicine, dentistry, law), but by 1991 that figure had risen to 39 percent;

Only 14 percent of all doctoral degrees went to women whereas in 1996 that figure had risen to 39 percent;

The medical degree earned during this period by women jumped from 8 percent to 39 percent, and by 1993 42 percent of first-year medical students were women;

Only 5 percent of women earned law degrees, but that figure in 1993 was 40 percent;

Women received only 1 percent of dental degrees compared to 32 percent by 1991;

In 1996, women earned the majority of the doctoral degrees awarded in pharmacy and veterinary medicine.

The summary concludes:

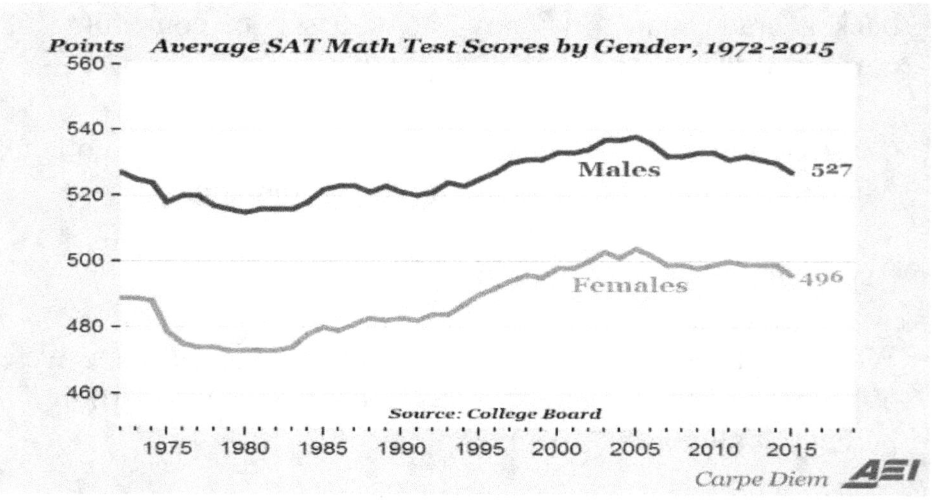

There is, however, a growing gender imbalance in higher education among minority students. Among black students who earned a bachelor's degree in 1990, fully 62 percent were female; among Hispanic students, 55 percent were female, and among white students, the imbalance was 53 percent to 47 percent favoring women.

FAST FORWARD TO THE 21ST CENTURY

The feminine resurgence is not only economic but cultural as well. To an amazing degree it mirrors the 11th, 12th, and 13th centuries (which will be covered in a future missive on *"The Ascent of the Working Woman"*) when the driver was not masculine but feminine dominance in manner, dress, speech, and decorum despite the prominence of the Crusades to the Holy Land during this period.

Today, we see much less evidence of the "glass ceiling," but now it is the mystical wall that seemingly blocks feminine progress if not feminine achievement. Statistics bear this out without the necessity of editorial comment.

As of 2015, the gender gap in favor of boys for mathematical aptitude across ethnic groups continues to persist. It is reflected in the Scholastic Aptitude (SAT) test where boys average higher math SAT scores than girls: 1.65 to 1.00, which has held for more than forty years. Girls, on other hand, during the same period, have continued to outperform boys on SATs for reading comprehension.

In 1994, 63 percent of female high school graduates and 61 percent of male high school graduates were enrolled in college. By 2012, the share of young women enrolled in college increased to 71 percent while 61 percent remained unchanged for the college enrollment of men.

On the other hand, a most recent report confirms that black women are the most educated group in the United States while being a long way from economic equity or social parity. Years 2009 to 2010, black women earned 68 percent of all associate degrees (two-year), as well as 66 percent of bachelor's degrees (four years), and 71 percent of master's degrees, and 65 percent of all doctorates.

Doctoral Degrees, By Field and Gender, 2015			
Field	Male	Female	Females per 100 Males
Arts and Humanities	47.6%	52.4%	110.1
Biological, Agricultural Sciences	47.6%	52.4%	110.1
Business	54.8%	45.2%	82.5
Education	32.1%	67.9%	211.5
Engineering	76.2%	23.8%	31.2
Health Sciences	30.3%	69.7%	230.0
Mathematics and Computer Sciences	70.6%	29.4%	41.6
Physical Sciences	64.8%	35.2%	54.3
Public Administration	34.5%	65.5%	189.9
Social, Behavioral Sciences	38.2%	61.8%	161.8
Other Fields	49.4%	50.6%	102.4
Total	48.2%	51.8%	107.5

Between 1976 and 2012, college students who were black increased from 10 to 15 percent, while the percentage of white students among U.S. college students fell from 84 to 60 percent. By both race and gender, a higher percentage of black women (9.7 percent) are enrolled in college than any other group, topping Asian women (8.7 percent), white women (7.1 percent), and white men (6.1 percent).

Most dramatic, where men once went to college far more than women – 58 percent to 42 percent – the ratio has now been nearly reversed. Today, women comprise more than 56 percent of all college students on college campuses nationwide. Some 2.2 million fewer men than women are enrolled in college today. *The new minority in American society is men.*

Postmodern Professional Men & Women Married to the Academic Factory DEGREE Machine System

As of 2010, the most popular master's degree for both men and women is the Master's Degree in Business Administration (MBA). Why this degree has such eminence is open to conjecture. There is some legitimacy for an MBA in the complexity of the corporate business world, but could this be hiding something, such as providing an anodyne for career anxiety?

From 1970 to 1980, I was an adjunct professor for several public and private universities (*The University of South Florida, Florida Institute of Technology, St. Petersburg College, St. Leo University, Nova University, Biscayne University,* and *Golden Gate University*) in which all these institutions presented the MBA degree to meet the demand. The motivation of the students was never clear other than to have an added bargaining chip for promotion. To put it another way, it was rare to find a student truly interested in management theory and thought to appreciate the efficacies, deficiencies, and embedded problems of the corporate culture.

Women were invariably the best MBA students for insight and pragmatic analysis of complex situations seldom becoming lost in the detail. No surprise, as of 2016, women have earned the majority of doctoral degrees every year since 2009 including in business curriculums.

Women started modestly, first earning the majority of the associate degrees in 1978, a majority of the master's degrees in 1981, and a majority of the bachelor's degrees in 1982.

As inflation is a common aspect of modern economic society, the bachelor's degree has proven the equivalent of a high school diploma in 1950. In 2015, realizing this, fully 26 percent of college graduates were back in school pursuing master's and doctorate degrees, mainly because of the pay gap between a BA and an MA degree.

Since all students, male and female, are likely married to the machine, the factory mentality and mindset have become endemic to the age. Good sense and rational appraisal of how cost-effective an advanced degree may be are seldom likely to be considered. The mantra is: *the bachelor's degree is meaningless if not worthless; therefore I must have an advanced degree.*

The growth of master's degrees

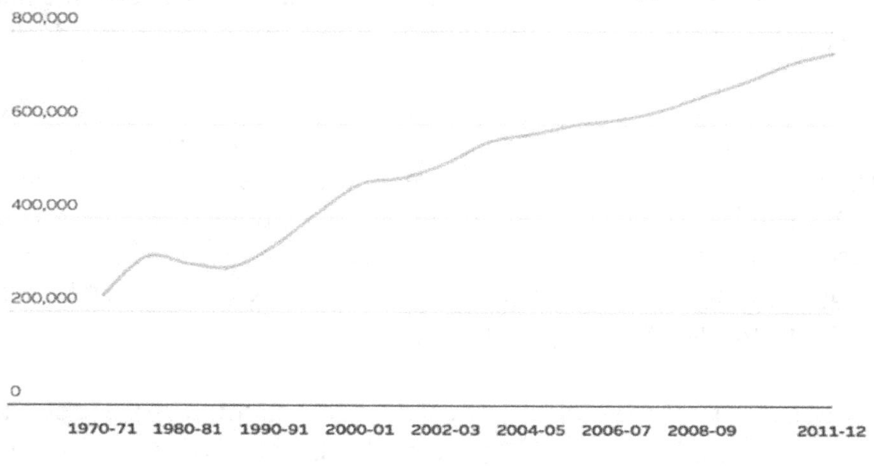

Against this rationale, the tuition for a master's degree at a public institution can be more than $30,000 a year, while at a private institution it can soar above $40,000 per year. Compare this with the average debt of $35,000 per college graduate with a bachelor's degree in 2015.

Then just how valuable is a master's or doctorate? Graduate degrees in science, technology, engineering, and mathematics command salaries from $68,000 to $117,000 whereas degrees of other disciplines (as will be soon shown) can be quite modest in comparison. Student loans can and often do plague college graduates for years into their working life. But new and surprising opportunities are evolving due in part to critical shortages in some professions.

New to the list is the physician assistant. This master's degree can earn $87,000 as median pay at the entry-level as of 2016. In the United States, largely because of the physician shortage, physician assistants are nationally certified and state-licensed to practice medicine under the supervision of a physician.

Graduate degrees in various areas of education, healthcare, and accounting can be far more modest in terms of possible income with an annual salary of $48,700. What is ironic is that professionals in such disciplines are most likely to be satisfied with their work despite the low paycheck.

BEST GRADUATE DEGREES FOR JOBS

Master's in Biostatistics: medium salary, $105,000

Master's in Statistics: $113,700

Ph.D., Computer Science: medium salary, $147,400

Ph.D., Economics: medium salary, $125,800

Master's in Applied Mathematics: medium salary, $124,900

Master's in Computer Science: medium salary, $125,700

Ph.D., Pharmacy: medium salary, $126,000

Ph.D., Mathematics: $106,600

Ph.D., Physics: $137,800

Master's Degree, Software Engineering: medium salary, $118,900

Ph.D., Physical Chemistry: medium salary, $134,800

Master's, Information Systems: medium salary, $116,100

Master's, Physician Assistant Studies: medium salary, $103,600

MBA, Management Information Systems: medium salary, $117,800

Ph.D., Political Science: medium salary, $116,700

WORST GRADUATE DEGREES FOR JOBS

Master's, Fine Arts (MFA): medium salary, $46,600

Master's, Early Childhood Education: $48,700

Master's, Divinity: $48,700

Master's, Elementary Education: $54,700

Master's, Reading & Literacy: $58,200

Master's, Theology, $57,800

Master's, Special Education: $59,200

Master's, Graphic Design, $72,700

Master's, Library and Information Science: $61,200

Master of Arts in Teaching: $60,100

Master's, Curriculum and Instruction: $60,600

Master's, Teaching English as a Second Language: $55,000

Master's, Pastoral Ministry: $60,800

Master of Architecture: $81,100

Master's, English Literature: $69,500

Then there is the persistent MYTHICAL WALL

Some sixty years ago when I was young, economic security, prestige, community respect, and unquestioned authority were the prerogative of the family physician. He didn't worry about lawsuits, or being disparaged by his clientele or worry about them second-guessing him. He was trusted as if a god to know and do what was best for everyone in his care without consideration of race, ethnicity, or economic circumstances.

That mystique, although severely tarnished, has survived to this day. It finds many women, as shown here, both black and white, making huge sacrifices to become physicians. The only problem is that being white instead of black tacks an extra $60,000 a year on the physician's paycheck if he is a man.

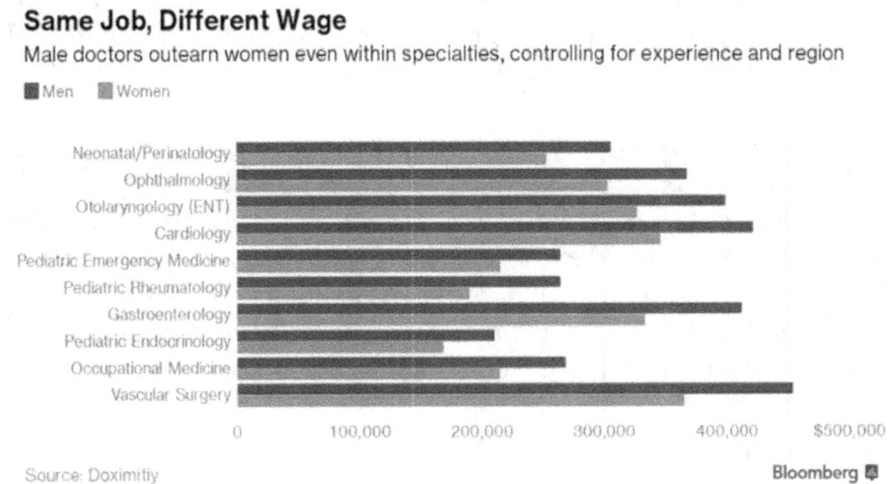

Medical doctors who are male earn 8 percent more than their female colleagues, which translates into $20,000 or more for the male physician doing the same work as the equally qualified female physician. The wage gap is so wide that women physicians teaching in medical schools as full professors make about the same as associate male professors.

This mythical wall was created more than one hundred years ago when there were few if any female doctors. The medical profession led by the American Medical Association created its brand as assiduously as

NFL owners created theirs. The AMA now defends that brand, believing itself indispensable if not the infallible authority on medical practice.

Indeed, the AMA promotes the correct dialogue with female doctors and claims to advocate equally the interests of female medical practitioners, but the gap between male and female doctors, and now the surging presence of black female physicians have continued to widen rather than shrink over the last several decades.

For white female physicians, this is not as pronounced a discrepancy as it is for black women physicians, but it does illustrate the fact that these highly qualified women of both races are pushing against a wall that although mythical remains a psychological and economic barrier that still holds these women in ascension from realizing their full potential and promise. It is as if the mystique that dominated my youth sixty years ago hangs on in its irrelevancy to this day.

The glass ceiling is gone, but this mythic barrier persists and it does so because medical patients today have the same mindset as patience fifty to one hundred years ago, and that is, believing that the white male doctor is omniscient when he is a disappearing phenomenon. The Ascent of the Working Woman *is in control of our creative tomorrow, establishing her essence without fanfare but with due diligence as this book attempts to illustrate.*

The Ascent of the Working Woman – 2nd edition, (2017) – Originally published in 1995 as The Worker, Alone! Going Against the Grain

"The Ascent of the Working Woman" is not new. The working woman was identified with a paradigm shift in the original "The Worker, Alone!" Women have been the measure of all things, especially our health and that of our community, doing so without power, using their guile to influence men when men were otherwise inclined. They have been forced to mainly be obliging listeners and supportive partners to men, who traditionally have the power. Whereas men, now mainly

professionals, but with women even outranking them in their quest for professional status, they have been systematically cutting the strings of restraining, and have not been inclined as with men to be managed, motivated, mobilized, and manipulated as it still blue-collar workers. When women acquire power they have been less inclined to "strut their stuff" in mocking imitation of male self-aggrandizement. That said, the working woman is equally capable of rational thinking and timely decision-making while married to the same antiquated economic and cultural machine.

PURPOSEFUL
SELLING
FOR THE 21ST CENTURY
It Starts with Creative Confidence
SECOND EDITION
Dr. James R. Fisher, Jr.

Setting Realistic Purposeful Goals

"The man without a purpose is like a ship without a rudder, a waif, a nothing, a no man. Have a purpose in life, and having it, throw such strength of mind and muscle into your work as God has given you."

Thomas Carlyle (1795-1881), British historian

The most important thing you have got to do is decide what you want to do. Once you've made that decision, the rest is easy."

These words were addressed to me by a friend. He is the owner and operator of a small publishing company. A few years ago he decided what he wanted. Since then, he has been making rapid progress in the direction of that goal. Publisher of a customized pricing service for the *Plumbing, Heating, and Air-Conditioning Industry,* he has allowed nothing to distract him from this purposeful objective.

His vocation and avocation have combined into a common drive. You could never meet a more dedicated or enthusiastic person at work. This man lives to work. One of the curious things about him, though, is that he is a terrific salesperson, but doesn't consider himself one.

To appreciate what an effective salesperson he is, consider a recent selling trip he took to Indiana, Illinois, and Kansas. He told me of his plans and what he expected to accomplish. Listening to him detail his plans with such enthusiasm was music to my ears, even if it taxed my rational mind.

One could not help but be impressed with the confidence in his voice, or the glint in his eye. He had worked hard to develop a good product, much needed in the industry. At the same time, he had made every effort to understand and anticipate the concerns of his customers and prospects alike. He knew their business and the operating problems that gave them fits, one of which was having out-of-date, inaccurate, and non-competitive pricing catalogs.

Quality driven to the extreme, nothing satisfies my friend until he is convinced his product *makes a difference,* helping his customer become competitive and, therefore, more successful. Such confidence is derived from knowing the customer's business as an insider; indeed, as a partner in the business.

As I studied him, I was certain no prospect underestimate his or her *added value.* Granted, it might take time to break through resistance barriers prospects construct. Not to worry. He saw this as part of the challenge of doing business. "If it were too easy," he would reflect, "the next person through the door would have my customer." "Resistance," he would cry in mock humor, "Viva la resistance!" Ultimately, the *area of the agreement* would bond them to the same purpose.

Ten days later he returned with enough business to require the addition of another permanent member to his staff. He accomplished exactly what he had planned. *My friend had not only planned correctly, but he had implemented his plan effectively.* Too frequently good planning suffers from poor implementation.

As much as I was impressed with this effort, I realized he had no doubt he would be successful. Then too, I knew every moment during that trip he was selling or thinking of selling. His whole being was concentrated on bringing home the business. So exceptional was his focus that it allowed little time for fear, worry, or negative interference of any kind. Nothing prevented him from channeling his energy to his purpose. Everything was working for him because he was in control.

The Cycle of Control

Being in control, my friend couldn't fail as his problem-solving powers had the correct frames of reference. The topography of the world of problem-solving is half a maze and half an obstacle course. Fortunately, there are some rules of thumb for getting started. A standard framework is a *content, context,* and *process:*

- *Content* is the problem subject matter. It means knowing your products and services from A to Z, and knowing your customer's business as an insider or partner.

- *Context* means the environment within which the problem-solving is conducted. For people in selling, this is a double-edged sword – *they must know their customer's working environment as well as their own.* The vital interest of both must be understood to be served. The situation can only be defined clearly if role demands and self-demands are under control. This involves knowing yourself (as well as the customer) in terms of beliefs and values. With the appropriate "toolbox" of social and technical skills, trusting relationships will be established by competent professionals.

- *The process* represents the problem-solving method or procedure. The process in the example above involved a field trip calling on key accounts with a well-planned selling agenda. The process is a road map with respective profiles of the contacts, histories of the business picture to date, specific presentations tailored to each customer's needs, and appropriate closes.

- The *Cycle of Control* starts with (1) *awareness* of the objective with major and minor goals; goes on with (2) *cognition* (awareness now aided by judgment); continues with (3) *diagnosis* (identifying the benefits to be derived from the product, service or idea presented against the current assessment of the needs); then describes (4) *viable alternatives* (realizing there is *never one best way* to do anything and that customers like options); follows this with (5) *selection* of the most appropriate action plan (consensus agreement between customer and seller); and then results in (6) *closure* and *implementation* (monitoring the process to ensure promised benefits). *The sale of anything begins with the order.*

This is a *Systems Approach to Selling,* which my friend organized without knowing. He was in touch with the power of his subconscious mind. Because his purpose was clear and his plan so well defined, he was able to do so with everything falling into place. *Systems thinking* has become a buzzword that can be misleading. For our purpose here the distinction we make with systems is that it has relatively clear and measurable boundaries. There is a positive synergy between buyer and seller because they see themselves as partners, not adversaries.

There is a tremendous amount of energy exhibited in the buyer-seller transaction. This energy is dynamic. Just as in chemistry, matter can be neither created nor destroyed, only transformed – the same applies at the end of the selling process – while the amount of energy remains the same, buyer and seller now differ in energy distribution. Both the seller and buyer are transformed (changed) by the process. Either the *buyer* is sold on the need for what the *seller* is offering, or the seller is sold by the buyer that no such need exists. In virtually every selling transaction *somebody is sold.* If the transaction does not yield the desired results, like chemistry, the process must be restudied in terms of *content, context,* and *process.* Not enough credit is given to the selling skills buyers demonstrate who refuse to buy.

Good solutions leverage the flux of energy to the seller. This edge gives the seller control of the process. Leveraging requires knowledge, cunning, and belief. Intelligence is the only advantage the seller has over the predictable problem. The flux and flow of energy during the sales interview must be understood to be exploited. Murphy thrives because human intuition about critical flux factors is wrong more often than right.

For example, had my friend's selling trip been deemed a failure, he would have taken little comfort in the inventions of failure. *Problem dodging* simply wasn't in his vocabulary.

Instead, a forthright *post-mortem* would follow in which he would assess the trip, bringing staff into the discussion. I am confident of this because that is what he did after this success. The debriefing involved two questions:

- What did I do that demonstrated how I can help our customers be more successful?

- What did I fail to do to demonstrate this value?

The questions seem quite harmless, but I was soon introduced to some *sensitive issues* as his staff took issue with him. A sample of this was the remarks of a printer.

"I'd like to turn those two questions around to us (here). We are your first customer, right? Well, you treat us fine, but none of us have ever been in the field. Some of us would even like to be trained in sales. We are not a one-man gang, are we? This has been brought up before, you know. You run this as your business, which it is, but we would like to get in on some of the action like you do. You know, none of us have ever seen a customer? I think that hurts when problems develop. We don't like to look stupid!"

I waited for his reply. Wow! I thought, what now? I was expecting anger or at least defensiveness. Instead, my friend paused, lit a cigarette, and smiled, nodding his head approvingly. Then he looked to the others waving his hand, palm up, to solicit their comment on the printer's assessment. Silence. He reminded them that their opinion was vital to operations. The silence continued.

Then he did a strange thing. He put two chairs in the center of the room, moving from chair to chair, talking to himself, as if the complaint of the printer had continued, and he and the printer were engaged in lively debate. In the role of the printer, he was quite hard on himself. As for himself, he kept probing for more information, for a better understanding of what was expected of him. Once the surprise subsided, this broke everyone up. After the laughter died down, he said simply, "Help me make us better." An open discussion followed. Imagine if all of us were filled with the spirit of my friend. We could:

- See ourselves as running our own business;
- Decide what we wanted to do and then do it;
- Think and expect success, finding no solace in *gonna dos and gonna buys;*
- Have that contagious confidence that puts people at ease;
- Embrace our problems as opportunities;
- Have such a confident grasp of our power that we would never have to flaunt it; and finally,
- Forget ourselves in work, worrying little about how things might appear to others.

Where are you, right now?

My friend did not experience such *togetherness* instantaneously. It came via a journey involving many false steps and a lot of pain. He once had a drinking problem and an unstable home life. When he hit bottom he decided to change directions and to have a purpose in his life. What about you? Where are you right now? Is it where you want to be? If not, understanding the *why* of your behavior could aid you in changing it for the better.

For our purpose, the *why* of behavior is built around work, but it could apply equally to home life. Salespeople notoriously dislike detail work, especially routine reports. The why of this behavior presents endless possibilities. They may:

- Not know they are required;
- Think they are not used and therefore not important;
- Not know how to do them;
- Have little interest in doing them;
- Feel they do not have time to do them;
- Think paperwork is not part of the job;
- Feel such activity is degrading.
- Unless you know why you resist part of your job, you are not in control.

Take another aspect of work, calling on large accounts versus small accounts. Perhaps you feel more confident in closing the small accounts. This is "the *what*" of behavior. Imagine you want to rise in the company, but you cannot see yourself *there*. When you ask yourself *why* in either of these examples, there are many possible explanations:

- You fear calls requiring you to enter the executive suite and make presentations before top people.
- You feel unable to cope with questions that arise from big accounts.
- You find more personal comfort in dealing with people in shirtsleeves while feeling intimidated by those in more formal attire.
- You may recall a personal failure in coping with a large account or may remember an embarrassing incident in a boardroom setting.
- You think *management* should handle big accounts and it should also manage your career.
- You like the certainty of quick gratification which is provided by the sale to a small account while disliking the extended business of building relationships at a large account with no guarantee of delayed gratification.
- You want the assurance that you will win promotion if you put forth more effort by accepting additional responsibility or going back to school.

Motivation is a complex problem. The behavior gives a good indication of what drives your performance. Only an honest appraisal, however, has any value to you.

Motives & Incentives

Understanding the difference between *motives* and *incentives* may prove helpful. Motives are the *driving forces within you* that make you behave as you do. *Incentives* are the *aspects of your environment that stimulate* you toward such efforts. For example, you may have a desire to become the director of your function (motive). Knowing that your company promotes from within could stimulate you to this end. What's more, you might know of several cases where people in sales moved up the organization more quickly than in other disciplines (incentive). Reflection on both motives and incentives is needed to gain an understanding of "the why" in our behavior.

In terms of *natural law,* every person to a varying degree wants to improve their performance and to taste success in what they do. When you see someone who defies this description, the forces of natural law, although distorted, are at work. We are all resilient, but there is a point when our driving forces become so stifled, our environment so repressive that we can lose our will to prevail. It can happen to any of us at any time in our lives. There is no safety zone from this possibility. Resilient as we are, we are also fragile. Our genetic selves need to feel that others care.

Result Expected versus Results Achieved

When we think of ourselves as efficient in all aspects of our work, we mean the *results achieved* equal to or exceed the *results expected* for the job. Likewise, when we see ourselves as inefficient, it means that in one or more job areas the results achieved are less than expected.

In the case of the latter this calls for another interpretation, a developmental view: Why am I not performing as well as I might?

Your buried assets must be brought to the conscious level. One of the peculiarities of being human is that we find it difficult to appreciate our assets (and yes, liabilities) until someone else tells us about them. Others see in us what we refuse to see or are unable to assess. This brings us to the matter of the fundamental characteristics of human personality.

Perceiving, Thinking & Feeling

If we are to gain an insight into the *why* of our behavior, we must ponder three interrelated continuous processes: *perceiving, thinking,* and *feeling.*

By perception, we mean the way we have of interpreting the people and things around us as we become aware of them through our senses. The meanings we attach to what we see, hear, taste, smell, and touch depend on our experience and our present state of mind and feelings. Perception is highly subjective. We tend to see what we want to see, hear what we want to hear. No two people witnessing the same event perceive it the same.

One of the major tasks in selling, as in all relationships, is to get the other person's perception of things, not ours. This includes a perception of how they see us. Only a trusted friend or a professional counselor or coach should be given such an invitation. Controlling the sales transaction demands that we harbor no false modesty or spurious expectations. We must *define the situation* accurately and realistically through every moment of the transaction. If we do, our perceptive skills are serving us well.

Thinking, on the other hand, involves a continuous interweaving of the experiential past and perceptual present. We use past experiences and present observations as grist for our mental mill. But this process, too, is influenced markedly by our state of mind and state of feelings. We have all observed occasions when we literally cannot think, our feelings disturbed, our minds distracted.

Feelings and emotions depend largely on our basic body chemistry and genetic code. Here, individual differences are observable. What triggers a favorable feeling in one person may leave a second person cold and a third person disturbed. Take an earthy joke for instance. One person may laugh heartily, another smile, still another frown. The intensity of our feelings is influenced by our temperamental make-up (body chemistry), our thoughts at that moment, and our surroundings. If we are to gain an insight into ourselves, we must discern what our feelings are and what we have on our minds. For example, when we feel ourselves becoming flush or our necks reddening, it is a good idea to take a "time out" and an inventory of our feelings. It is amazing how much anguish can be avoided if we take but the sixty-second break from emotional frenzy to examine what is happening to us and why.

Take the case of the outstanding technical salesperson who was vehemently attacked by a customer for a systems failure. Later, it was demonstrated that the fault had nothing to do with the salesperson's product. It was deduced that an electrical storm had knocked out the main generator for several predawn hours which had caused the problem. Unfortunately, the salesperson, once the attack became personal, stood up and said in a husky voice.

"You have insulted me, sir. Speaking man to man, I don't have to take that from you or anyone else. Good day!"

The customer, known as a bully, was astonished. He sat speechless with his chief engineer and production manager. He was embarrassed. But he got the last word, changing suppliers' posthaste. Then, as destiny would have it, he moved rapidly up the hierarchy to top management. Never forgetting this brazen affront, he systematically eliminated this salesperson's company from its privileged position as a principal supplier. Ultimately, more than a million dollars' worth of business was lost because this salesperson could not control his feelings.

Personality & Adjustment Skills

The core of our personality is our character, our *life value system.* Here is the depository of the good-bad, the right-wrong, the do's-not do's, the beautiful-ugly that affect our attitude toward people and things. Our *life values* influence and provide a *frame of reference* for making choices. It is difficult for us to know our character directly and impossible for others. We reveal ourselves when we express our attitudes and make choices. What we say is often misleading, but our behavior seldom lies.

Let us say a person misuses the company car. When told this, the person sees nothing wrong with what they did. This infers a distortion in their value system. Should the person acknowledge the misuse, we would infer from this that their values were undistorted but that they lacked the knowledge of proper maintenance. The abuse is correctable.

If your value system is socially and morally acceptable, but there are shortcomings in your behavior which you would like to correct, this book can help develop and improve your *adjustment skills.*

We have heard the expression, often given in jest, "You need a personality adjustment." All of us require adjustment from time to time. Our most desirable behavior is characterized by purposefulness and efficiency. This is expressed when we have certain goals, and we desire to pursue them with a minimum waste of time and energy. When obstacles arise or we are distracted from our intended purpose, our *positive adjustment skills* come into play.

Changing careers, once frowned upon, has become a popular method of *positive adjustment.* How about you? Have you made similar career adjustments? If not, would you like to? Is this discussion helping you to make such career decisions?

Experts say that the average person will have five to six career changes in the span of their working life. This means that realistic goal setting is not written in concrete. Your life is an entire quilt. Each experience (and career) is a piece of cloth, which when added to the quilt, can be something beautiful to behold.

On a pragmatic basis, a salesperson may find they constantly reset their sights, modifying or changing their goals, from sales call to sales call. Frequently this means settling for less. For example, on a particular sales call they may have set as their target the closing with a quantity order. As they proceed, they realize that a trial order is more realistic. When they make this adjustment, taking the pressure off the buyer to make a big commitment "now versus later," they create a win-win situation. Meanwhile, a successful trial gives the buyer ammunition to justify the changeover.

Many of us would like to be entrepreneurs. It sounds exciting, even romantic and challenging. Challenging it is. . . as it requires risk-taking, venturing capital, sacrificing, and spending long hours in laborious detail work. The romantic picture dissolves for some when faced with this crushing reality. *Positive adjustment,* in this case, involves the recognition that security carries more importance than its twin, uncertainty. And that is okay. There is no point in being an adventurer if you prefer being a sidewalk superintendent.

Sometimes, instead of modifying our goals, it is more constructive to *change our approach* to them. This is another method *of positive adjustment.* Suppose you have great ideas but lack the risk-taking bravado of the entrepreneur. You could persuade management to allow you to create skunkworks™ with other specialists to work on specific projects critical to the success of the company. In your sales presentation (believe me, this is selling!) to convince management to support your idea, you could weave into the discussion such notables as Tom Peters and William L. Livingston, both of whom make great cases for skunkworks™.

Skunkworks™, incidentally, represent bands of five to ten zealots off in a corner often out-producing product development groups that number in the hundreds.

On the other hand, a salesperson might find they are making little progress calling on the purchasing agent because the general manager makes all major buying decisions. Keeping the same goal in mind, you could ask the purchasing agent to act as your emissary in setting up a meeting with the general manager.

When circumstances interfere with our purposeful performance we sometimes adjust negatively to the obstacles which arise. One such *negative adjustment* is to direct our attention to the interference and away from the goal. We attack the person or thing in our path *(direct aggression),* or we take out our feelings on someone or something else *(displaced aggression)*. An example of direct aggression would be losing our temper with a customer because of what we consider unreasonable demands, either on our person (self demands) or the company (e.g., on pricing policy). Should such a salesperson return to the office after an unsuccessful day and be abusive to the secretary, this would illustrate displaced aggression.

Another *negative adjustment* involves *withdrawing* into ourselves. In this case, you refuse to face the situation. Both goal and obstacle become cloudy. The person who sulks in the face of problems illustrates this form of adjustment.

In addition to *aggression* and *withdrawal,* there is a third method of negative adjustment, *retreat*. Some people, when frustrated, run away from the obstacle and forget the goal. The salesperson who fails to call back after a flat refusal illustrates adjustment by retreat.

The well-adjusted person makes one of the three positive adjustments most of the time under most circumstances. Only occasionally do they adjust negatively. In contrast, the maladjusted individual often adjusts negatively to the environment. Our challenge, as individuals, is to gain insight into our *life value system* to understand the personality adjustments we make and why we make them. If we can do this, we will have our lives under control with confidence radiating from this control. Moreover, we will be able to accomplish whatever we set our minds to accomplish.

In short, we have learned that setting purposeful and realistic goals involves understanding ourselves. Impulsively setting goals on paper has little to do with how we perceive, think, and feel. That is why we are constantly correcting our goals to better match our natures and desires. In that connection, we are now aware of the difference between motives and incentives, and how our core personality and character relate to the way we make choices and adjust to the circumstances we experience. The power of our subconscious mind is released when we experience ourselves as we are. In the chapter which follows we will explore in greater detail the *why* of our behavior and the important place confidence has in our selling success.

"You are your own worst enemy!" we have heard most of our lives, and also, "The first friend you must make is that with yourself!" If this is true, then why is self-realization so difficult and self-defeat so much more attractive? It is a matter of confidence.

If you are truly committed to exploring this dilemma, this book is for you. It explores such questions as:

Why are we our own worst enemy?

Why do many of us fail to find fulfillment in our lives and vocations?

Why is 80% of *purposeful performance* in most organizations accomplished by 20% of the workforce?

Why do 10% lead while 90% choose to follow?

Why do most of us not have the slightest notion of a purpose in life?

Why do so few of us ever challenge our true potential?

Why do we torture ourselves with doubts, while giving others the benefit of the doubt?

Yes, indeed, why, why, why?

It would seem, at first blush, a matter of fear – unmitigated, incomprehensible fear. This corrosive and destructive humor eats into a person's mind, making them ill-tempered and likely to act uncharacteristically – behavior which neither love nor success will condone or confidence support.

As apparent as fear is, less obvious is that of *comfort* and *complacency.* These are cultural hazards inspired by having it too good for too long. Insulated from reality, such persons think showing up for work on time and doing what they are told is enough to satisfy their existence. That saying "I love you" in personal relationships is enough to fulfill the demands of commitment. Not so, for the products of *comfort* and *complacency* are purposeless behavior, negative thinking, and psychological inertia. This leads to the destruction of self-confidence and results in everything being suspect.

Look around you. Do you think the people *making it happen* are more talented than you? Are they more able and experienced, better trained, or more knowledgeable? Do you suppose they have more confidence? If they are not truly better, what, then, makes them stand out?

They choose to accept themselves as they are and others as *they find them.* They don't own other people's problems, only their own. And they take them head-on. Moreover, they choose to have fun at work and in life. They choose to take the great gift of life seriously, but not themselves. That allows them the latitude of philosophically taking the fortunate with the unfortunate. They accept that life is an eternal struggle. There is no growth without the need for embracing the possibility of failure or embarrassment. Life, love, and success are part of the same whole – a journey, not an end.

On balance, it requires each of us to be brutally honest with and about ourselves. How about you?

Are you *aware* of who you are, where you are, how you got there as opposed to where you would like to be?

Do you fully *accept* yourself as you are?

Do you have *confidence* in such knowledge?

Or do you pretend to yourself, as you would to others, to being someone else?

Purposeful Selling is founded in:

- Self-knowing;
- Understanding why;
- Tolerating our inevitable ineptitude;
- Showing compassion for ourselves as well as others;
- Giving us an insight into our dilemma and the tools for doing something.

This book is designed to be a companion to you as you meet these challenges in your personal and professional life. In that sense, it is a private counselor, a morale booster, a prospective giver, allowing you to see yourself and your situations more clearly.

Always have it at hand to remind you that you are not alone in this *crisis in confidence.* Don't let the confident masks we all like to wear in public fool you. We are all brothers and sisters under the skin, susceptible to the same doubts and misgivings as you.

But the monkey on your back is not my monkey. I can neither knock your monkey off your back nor can you knock my monkey off mine. Good luck to you in *monkey bashing* from someone who is still busy knocking his private monkeys for a loop

Purposeful Selling for the 21st Century, 2nd Edition (2014) – Originally Confident Selling for the 90s (1992)

Purposeful Selling was nominated for a Pulitzer Prize for nonfiction in its first edition. The book introduced a new paradigm in the selling equation showing the seller and the buyer as partners, not adversaries in the exchange as they were engaged in creative problem-solving.

PURPOSEFUL
SELLING
FOR THE 21ST CENTURY
It Starts with Creative Confidence
SECOND EDITION
Dr. James R. Fisher, Jr.

From the 2nd edition of SIX SILENT KILLERS (2014)

Times have changed. Downsizing, rightsizing, reengineering, corporate restructuring, and merging have drastically altered the physical, psychological, and cultural face of the American workplace. Yet, most managers are still using the same dated methodology of dealing with employees that would appear fixated with the structure and function of work dating back to the end of World War Two. This has predictably resulted in disastrous results. "Six Silent Killers" reveals how this has incrementally occurred leading workers to collective dissatisfaction, apathy, and counterproductive behavior.

Six Silent Killers:

Written in user-friendly personal and empirical terms by a recognized leader in the field.

Illustrates the most effective methods of handling employee-management relations of an essentially professionally trained workforce.

Shows how to establish an effective and sustainable Culture of Contribution where professionals are treated as partners with management, not as subordinates.

Provides an in-depth analysis of atavistic managers and an anachronistic organizational structure and how to reposition the complex organization so that everyone is on the same page and getting off on the same dime.

Encourages managers and professionals to embrace rather than deny the sudden and compelling shift from "position power" to "knowledge power" where workers as professionals now hold the key to organizational success.

MANAGEMENT'S GREATEST CHALLENGE
Dr. James R. Fisher, Jr

From the pages of the 2nd edition of SIX SILENT KILLERS (2014)

WHY AMERICANS CAN'T GET THEIR WORK DONE!

Asking the Right Questions!

In 2001, I performed an intervention at the Children's Board of Hillsborough County in Tampa, Florida, an agency that delivers important services to indigent children in the county. I asked the director, "What do you want me to do?"

The director answered, "Find out why we can't get our work done." Subsequently, I used that title in my report: *Why the Children's Board of Hillsborough County Can't Get Its Work Done.*

It was the right question. The report was a forensic study of what went wrong and why, and how to correct these deficiencies. When it was finished, however, the director was so incensed with my report she short-changed me $3,600 as retribution for answering a politically incorrect question.

In 2012, she was removed from her office and a high-octane local politician and former mayor, Pam Iorio, took over in an interim capacity, implementing many of the recommendations made in my report. She also reduced administrative staff and field operatives by nearly one-third. Iorio has organizational skills and an instinct for doing the right thing, along with political clout.

Powering Out

The question of why Americans can't get their work done has been a concern of mine since 1980. Before that time, I operated either in the field or as a top executive, never having worked professionally in the bowels of the corporation.

After earning my Ph.D. in 1977, I consulted for many Fortune 500 companies, finally joining one in 1980, Honeywell, Inc. in Clearwater, Florida as a management and organizational development psychologist. We conducted several studies between 1980-1986 dealing with work efficiency. As a result, I identified six passive individual behaviors and three dominant corporate cultures. In the process, I discovered many functional groups were performing at levels of organizational efficiency about 50% of what was expected.

Later, in 1986, as the director of organizational development for Honeywell Europe Ltd., the efficiency of Honeywell workers in Europe proved to be about the same as in the U.S. with clear signs of the same passive behaviors and cultures.

By 1990, it was clear to me why the United States and Europe were failing to get their work done. These observations were followed up with a series of articles and books, *Six Silent Killers* (1998) being the most comprehensive.

Now, in the 21st century, with the advent of powerful personal IT devices, distracting from as much as contributing to work, while worker efficiency continues to plummet. The irony is, with the power of these electronic devices soaring, individual worker efficiency is becoming increasingly irrelevant, leading to the conclusion that humans may be factoring themselves out of existence, somewhat as drone technology is in the process of revolutionizing boots on the ground warfare. Asking the right question doesn't seem natural to us.

Right Question Overruled

In 2003, the United States in a heightened state of fear and paranoia following the New York City Twin Towers terrorist attack of September 11, 2001, the wrong question was asked of Iraq: where are the weapons of mass destruction (WMDs), when the right question should have been are there WMDs in Iraq?

Ambassador Joseph C. Wilson wrote a series of articles in The New York Times debunking the Niger intelligence claims that uranium sales were made to Iraq, which President George W. Bush misrepresented in his State of the Union address leading up to the pre-emptive invasion of Iraq.

General Colin Powell, with CIA Director George Tenet sitting behind him as he addressed the United Nations, laid out a case of Iraq having these phantom WMDs. It became a burlesque comedy of tragic proportions. Wilson was maligned, and his wife, the covert CIA operative Valerie Plame, was exposed and compromised, all this from asking the wrong question.

No Contest

Six Silent Killers doesn't ask: "Where are these passive behaviors?" Rather, it asks the more audacious question: what sponsors these collective behaviors, and what are we doing about it?

These killing behaviors exist undetected negating productive effort in two of these three dominant workplace cultures:

The Culture of Comfort is management dependent with the manager acting as a surrogate *parent* to reactive and taciturn workers;

The Culture of Complacency finds workers counter dependent on the organization for their total well-being suspended in the terminal adolescence of the dependent *child*; and

The Culture of Contribution departs from this dependence with workers and managers cooperating and collaborating as partners in the enterprise in mature *adult* relationships.

While the *Culture of Complacency* may thrive in some quarters in 2013, surely the "six silent killers" operate even more so in work cultures and industries plagued by constant restructuring, mergers & acquisitions, downsizing, and/or divisive and incompetent leadership.

The managerial class has been waging a losing war against workers for nearly three decades, and it continues, now aided by state and federal governments. Despite apparent gridlock and dysfunction, corporate society persists in *business as usual* practices and the exercise of infallible institutional authority while ignoring the mounting evidence of the corporate decline in forwarding inertia.

The right question to ask is how much longer can the United States afford this?

Some 24 states in the United States have now passed union-busting legislation, calling it "Right to Work" legislation. This has been in part driven by the impossibility of states being able to maintain the funding of their benefit and retirement plans. It is not uncommon in the State of California, for example, to retire with a yearly income (including benefits) in the range of $100,000 to $200,000. The mean average is in the range of $40,000 per year for 60 percent of state retirees, which is well above the national average of industrial retirees. Who pays for these exorbitant compensation packages? Taxpayers do! Keep this in mind.

Delay of the Game

Symptoms of the problem are evident everywhere. Currently, our attention is drawn to the National Hockey League's owners' contract impasse with the players association (NHLPA). It has been finally resolved but after canceling half of the current 2012-2013 NHL season. The long-term contract should keep peace in this sport for the next eight or ten years, that is, with players and owners, but what about fans? It is yet to be learned what are the long-term consequences of this most contentious struggle between labor and management. Neither complacency nor the six silent killers are easily detected as they represent a mindset that feels it is being taken advantage of, which translates into justifying negative behavior. Little or no concern is paid to the unintended consequences. What might they be?

The wrong question for NHL players was why did they refuse to settle when the right question is how much longer will NHL fans be able to afford to continue to pay the high price for supporting the sport?

Owners know there is a limit to how long they can continue to sign high-priced player contracts without exceeding the ability of ticket buyers to pay. Players want more revenue, and many fans are on their side, without those fans or players knowing the price of doing business other than the sport's entertainment value. The business risks are outside their purview. Typically, professionals of all stripes, when asked about such factors as business risks, reply without hesitation, "That's not our problem," when it is everyone's in the long run.

The other right question is why is there so much distrust between players and owners, workers and managers? Inappropriate questions are asked because of false assumptions.

When Greed Became Good...

During the golden era of business in the 1950s, 1960s, and 1970s, that is, before the rest of the world caught up with the United States competitively, the differential in compensation between workers and managers was modest. The differential climbed in the 1980s, soared in the 1990s, and has spiraled beyond comprehension in the 21st century.

It is no accident that the *Six Silent Killers* became prevalent in the 1990s when "greed became good."

It is the reason the "Occupy Wall Street" (OCW) movement was launched without an apparent agenda, but with pervasive frustration and confusion as 1% of the population was said to earn or control wealth equivalent to what the bottom 90 percent generated with which to live. OCW didn't know what question to ask so they simply acted as squatters, expressing their indignation.

Another wrong question to ask is what can management do about this waste when the right question is when will workers tire of being disenfranchised from the workplace, from the money changers, and the marketplace? When will they realize they stir the drink?

An ancillary right question would be: what prevents workers from growing up and accepting responsibility and accountability consistent with their interests? It is futile to look for demons.

There are no demons here, no good guys and bad guys, only workers, and managers moving away from good sense and the pragmatics of the *psychology of William James*, where self-interest once trumped everything as it mutually served workers and managers alike.

Ultimate Questions

To put things in perspective, more than 90% of what workers demanded at the beginning of the last century — a safe and healthy working environment, pay for performance, social benefits, adequate vacations, and opportunities for promotion — has essentially been given to them.

Six Silent Killers is not about powerless workers under siege using passive behaviors to justify their frustration in the workplace. Nor is it about anachronistic management, which is outdated, but which, paradoxically, is supported and sustained daily by passive workers and reactive managers. Neither workers nor managers want to face up to the struggle necessary to establish a new system, which would appease if not eliminate the litany of complaints about "the system," as well as their angst with each other. Who is the system: everyone!

Countless attempts have been made over time to encourage workers to self-manage, including putting them on salary and giving them professional status. I don't know of a single case where hourly workers voted to sacrifice the possibility of overtime pay to work beyond their shift or on a Saturday or Sunday without additional compensation, as is the case with most professional workers. Opportunity doesn't seem to be enough.

The final question, which the reader might ask is not why workers are suspended in adolescence, but when will they escape this dependence, and decide to "grow up"? A secondary question: when will workers realize they can work without managers?

Today's workplace is experiencing change at a breathtaking pace. Before our eyes, opportunities are growing exponentially. What's less obvious is that the road ahead is booby-trapped. If we're going to move forward, the biggest change of all will have to be in the maps we draw for ourselves—in how our culture chooses to define value and contribution.

In my 40 years of work experience, I've held jobs in every type of organization and came away with viscerally etched memories of the trials and tribulations of trendy management. I've had countless front-line adventures amid the rants and ravings of management gurus, from classical management theory to the new age. I've heard the old songs of company loyalty, have sung a few of my own, and have listened to incantations about the soul from people who champion "value-added" gratuitously until you ask them what it means. Even guru Michael Hammer, whose *Re-Engineering the Corporation* is credited with starting an avalanche of corporate layoffs, is not exempt from rethinking his position. In the aftermath of his book's success, Hammer (sometimes called the father of downsizing) reportedly suggested he wasn't smart enough in his advice about the people equation, that his book over reflected his engineering background. Great. Imagine an engineer suffering the over-influence of his discipline. The people who constitute the human equation are the ones who felt the brunt of it.

Scott Adams' cartoon character Dilbert reminds us daily of the importance of the human equation, but corporations continue handing out pink slips, even when doing so cuts into the muscle of their organizations. They don't know what else to do to positively affect their quarter's profits, even when the knowledge in the heads of workers is their most valuable asset. Because the bottom line and the human equation have never been parallel considerations, the results now seem out of kilter.

Philosopher & novelist **Charles D. Hayes** writes of author Fisher:

One thing is certain; the time for well-intentioned fads is over. And a short-term-profit mentality at the expense of longer-term strategies for survival is an assurance that a business will not endure. We have one foot on the front step of a global marketplace which promises more change in the next decade than we have experienced in the past half-century in terms of how we earn our living. Our other foot is tiptoeing reluctantly toward the new millennium—a time of exaggerated flux which exacerbates human anxiety by design, an era when pessimists pronounce the end of everything and optimists the reverse. In times like these, organizations and political groups attempt to leverage insecurity by scapegoating easy targets. Such times call not for gurus, but for people who see clearly. We need keen observers like James R. Fisher, Jr.

In a style reminiscent of Ralph Waldo Emerson, Fisher's vibrant prose packs more purpose into a paragraph than most writers achieve in a whole chapter. Emerson was the architect who laid the groundwork for the contemporary thesis "what goes around comes around." In his essay titled "Compensation," he said, "Every excess causes a defect; every defect an excess . . . For every grain of wit, there is a grain of folly . . . Every advantage has its tax." Similarly, Fisher shows how every action taken in the modern business world has consequences, both good and bad. He portrays today's organizational reality with striking precision and clarity. It's a reality you will recognize immediately if you have a long work record, and one you dare not ignore if you lack experience.

James Fisher shares with self-taught social critic Eric Hoffer a talent for making provocative observations that burst the bubbles of popular opinion. The silent killers he writes about here represent the residue of obsolete job culture. They harken back to a mechanical era that served its purpose well, but one which Fisher makes obvious cannot be sustained. The velocity of change we are experiencing renders current knowledge increasingly obsolete exactly at a time when we are witnessing the unraveling of the expert. The lock on knowledge customarily held by institutions and "experts" is giving way to individual initiative. What you know is rapidly becoming more important than who you know.

My prescription is to think of education, not as something you get but something you take. Fisher asserts that all real education is self-education, that disaster awaits those who leave it to others to define value. Those who hope to latch their "destiny to another's rainbow" will find nothing solid to grasp and a total absence of reward at the end.

In Six Silent Killers: Management's Greatest Challenge, James R. Fisher, Jr. offers compelling insights into how we can move from a culture of comfort and complacency to a culture of contribution. This is not a simple task. There are no easy exits or off-ramps. The road to genuine contribution is steep, crooked, pot-holed, and sometimes full of land mines. Visibility is obscured; the greatest danger might occur when the road appears smooth and straight. It's a sign of the times that no one can mark your map for you, whether you are a CEO, a middle manager, or a line worker. But James R. Fisher, Jr. is a guide whose acute observations from the trenches of international corporate life offer a kind of wisdom seldom found in books about management. If you pay the price of attention, he will help you chart your path to the future.

Meet Your New Best Friend, 2nd Edition (2013) – Originally The Taboo Against Being Your Own Best Friend (1996)

"Meet Your Own Best Friend" shows the reader that we are all authors of our footprints in the sand, heroes of the novels inscribed in our hearts. Everyone's life is sacred, unique, a scripted high drama played out before an audience of one with but one actor on stage. The sooner we realize this the more quickly we overcome the bondage of loneliness and find true friendship with ourselves.

To attempt to do for others what they best do for themselves is to weaken their resolve and diminish them as persons. The same holds for us.

To have a friend you must be a friend starting with yourself. This is a simple declarative statement of a fact that is seldom recognized in the philosophical dictum of interpersonal relationships, or indeed, in social intercourse in general. Too often friends are sought to enhance self-tolerance which becomes the magnate of social interaction.

No greater taboo exists in society to consider oneself first and one's own best friend. Throwing off the chains of this illusion is nigh impossible because there is little precedence or tolerance for such self-regard. It is considered narcissistic and selfish when it is virtually impossible to be a friend to anyone if that friendship is not derivative of self-regard.

True acceptance of others as we find them is not possible without self-acceptance. In the past, work drove deeds, now deeds drive work.

We now live in the Information Age with Artificial Intelligence in an absurd if not an obscure attempt through social media to replace individualism with the community as if the premodern self differs from the postmodern self. This finds Amazon, Google, Apple, and Microsoft designers, among others, engaged in replacing conscience, consciousness, tolerance, and integrity with a virtual identity where humanity and self-regard are anachronistic. *"Meet Your New Best Friend"* clearly is of another mind.

SECOND EDITION
Meet Your New Best Friend
ADD AS A FRIEND
Dr. James R. Fisher, Jr.

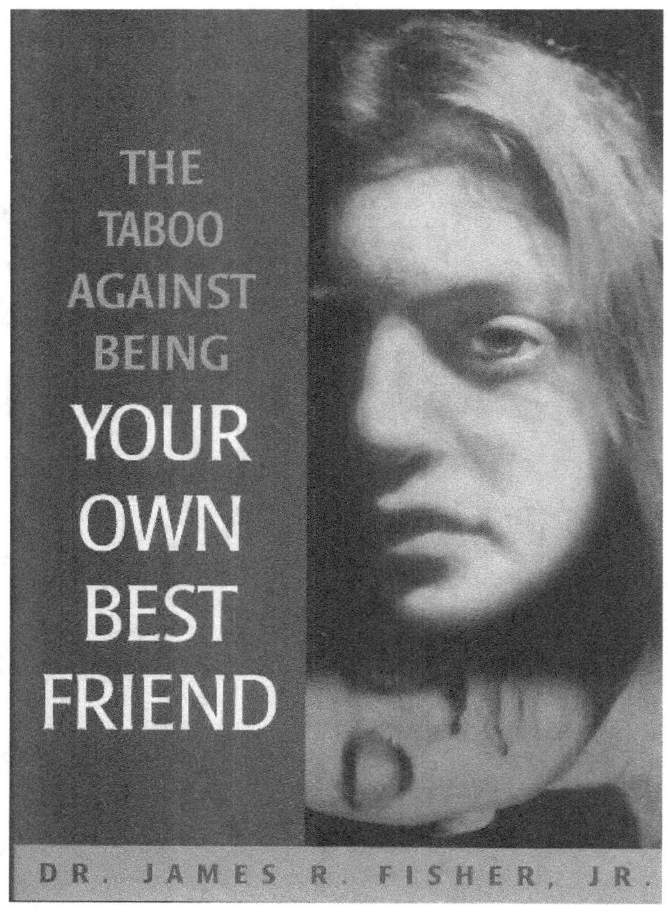

From the pages of BEING YOUR OWN BEST FRIEND (2013)

Walking the Tightrope & Avoiding the Traps

It is a lifelong struggle from childhood through adolescence to maturity to establish a career, a relationship with significant others, and then should you have children, to go through the whole process again.

Often, we do to our children what has been done to us. We put a monkey on their backs that were put on ours. We create the same self-doubt in them that was created in us.

We blame ourselves while growing up by second-guessing what we should and should not do, spending little time to understand why we desired what we did. It is a monkey circus we play on ourselves.

Like a spinning top, our life can spin out of control and come to rest exactly where it started without interruption or insight, denying us the freedom to experience life to the fullest. Or we can become obsessively concerned with always looking over our shoulders to see if someone is watching or chasing us.

I have a friend who has had a very successful career. He was at the top of his class in high school and college, successful financially and professionally. One day we met after a separation of nearly fifty years for breakfast at the *Country Kitchen Restaurant* of our hometown. Looking at him across the breakfast nook, I noticed his eyes had a haunting sadness that suggested a misspent life. This seemed incongruous, so I asked him how he was.

"Fine," he replied, but his eyes told another story. He asked me the same. *"Okay,"* I replied with a smile and shrug. *"What can I say, I'm an old man still struggling to grow up?"*

"You don't look like you're struggling at all," he said, obviously a compliment that stopped me.

"You think?" Could he envy me? Not possible! Thinking of that, I added, *"Don't kid yourself, I'm still struggling to climb my mountain, or is it only a hill?"* It was meant to lighten the discourse but failed.

He looked at me with a seriousness I remembered of him. *"I always knew you'd be a writer."* I waited. *"You know how I knew?"* Again, I waited. *"My mother told me. Remember that time you had that long conversation with her?"* I did. *"She came to me afterward, and said, 'Mark my words, that boy is going to be a writer.' Did you know that?"*

"No, but I remember our talk. It was the only time I ever spoke to her." I grew thoughtful recalling the incident. He had asked me to be his college roommate. The conversation with his mother was an interview to determine my acceptability. His parents didn't know me, or my parents. Their paths had never crossed at church or the country club.

Their boy was an outstanding student and a good Protestant. I was this tall, blond kid who played sports, and rumor had it, was Catholic. It was not difficult to imagine their concerns.

"Your mother loaned me a book," I continued with a grin, *"and I never returned it. That was not the most auspicious move on my part."*

"Em? She never said."

"Well, she did, and I'll tell you something else, the book proved prophetic."

"How so?"

"It was Alan Paton's Too Late the Phalarope. I read the book, reread it, and practically memorized it, and still have it." My mind turned dreamy thinking about the book's imagery. The phalarope is a small shore bird like a sandpiper. In the story, it found itself in Johannesburg, more than 400 miles from the sea. Who would have thought one day I would find myself a young executive in South Africa living in Johannesburg far from my cultural moorings of Iowa and the Mississippi River? In my South Africa experience, I was to learn how powerful culture and climate can act on one's character. I could identify with Pieter Van Vlaanderen in Paton's story.

Mentioning the book caused a sunshine smile to break across his stoic countenance. I could tell he loved his mother. But it turned to shale when I said, *"You look a lot like your father now."*

I could see he had the same conflicting memory of his father I had of mine. His father was an executive, brilliant engineer, and my da was never invited into that success club. I could see why my friend had been successful, but why had I? Where did my drive come from? Could it be the quick start I got mimicking his study habits? God, how he cracked the books! He didn't just study a subject; he devoured it. I watched this in amazement. He didn't make love to a subject, he raped and ravished it as if it was something he hated but needed to possess. I think I lacked his passion. My concern was the fear of flunking out, of being caught the stupid person I was, the fraud, the pretender, the flake, the jock. Many nights I would lie in my bed hearing the gentle rhythm of his breathing across the room. He slept the good sleep knowing the day had belonged to him. He had conquered it and held dominion over it. Then there was me. I slept fitfully, wondering if I would survive the week. I could envision myself an early Christian ascetic prostate on the steps of the cathedral in wanton humility. I was messed up. My Catholicism was my disease.

In high school, we had known each other but not well. He was at the top of the class and I barely made the top ten percent. Now in college, because we were both gunners, we were in the upper three percent of our class of 2,000 male students, courtesy of the United States Selective Service "Draft Board's" statistics.

The Korean War, a war never declared by Congress, was going on. Classmates were dropping out and resurfacing in Korea all the time. Every six months, we would be reclassified with our class ranking. We knew everybody above us with these rankings. I think one of the reasons he accepted me was the fact that I was among them, obviously below him of course.

When you are college roommates, and see each other every day, I suppose you are bound to be surprised. Mine was to find he had doubts and insecurities, too, but with a difference. He expected to succeed. It was obvious there was no doubt in his mind. I've come to believe in sociobiology, the idea that there is something genetic to one's psychology, anthropology, and physiology.

I remember reading *The Secret Diary of Harold L. Ickes* (1953), who was *Secretary of Interior* in *President Franklin D. Roosevelt's administration*. Ickes tells of an incident where the president as a young student at Harvard put his drunken friend on a train with $10 in his pocket and a ticket to the West Coast. Ten years later the president's friend was a millionaire. Of course, his father was already one, so it was in his genes, just as it is in the genes of baseball players' sons to become major leaguers.

One time we had studied late at the library on a frigid Iowa night with the temperature hovering around zero degrees Fahrenheit. My friend stopped in the middle of the bridge of the Iowa River dividing the campus. Steam was pouring out of his stocking cap and his breath was a flume of icy molecules, and said, "Imagine what they would say tomorrow if we should perish in this icy river tonight." Stumping my feet to put some circulation into them, and pushing my hands deeper into my mackinaw, I must confess I thought he had gone a little mad.

Undaunted, he continued with rhetorical glee, "They would say, think," dramatic pause, "what they might have been?" Well, now we know. No big deal.

The fact that he included me in the "they," at the time, was a little overwhelming, but all my cold mind could rev up was that "they" would say I couldn't hit the curveball.

Thinking about that night now, with the perspective of 50 years, I realized what a huge mountain he had given himself to climb. What was sad to see, successful a climb as he had made, is that it seemed to have given him so little satisfaction. It made me think of the Peggy Lee song, *"Is that all there is to love?"*

My mountain was more like rolling hills, the difference between the landscape say, of Florida and Colorado. Quite remarkably, he confessed to having never failed. I admitted to a lifetime of bumps in the road. I kidded, *"In my life's Monopoly Game, the card I keep drawing says go back to start."*

It was true. Every time I was heading for the high rent district, something intervened, setting me back. Also true, it was often by choice not wanting to compromise. Some might say it was my hardheaded stupidity, and they may be right, but I never felt too bad about going back and starting over.

Sitting across from me now, it appeared he envied me. He wanted to know more about my life, but in particular about me, the writer. *"Has anyone ever told you there is an aura about you?"*

"I don't know what you mean." Had he gotten weird, too?

"Let me put it bluntly. You look like the success that I've had. How do you explain that?"

This made me roar with laughter, causing other people to look our way. I have a deep-throated laugh that shakes a building's foundation. *"If I didn't know better, I'd feel a con coming on."*

"I mean it."

"Listen! You've had a great life, a major success, been one of those stratospheric contributors to the university, hell, they could call you a philanthropist."

"Hardly."

"Okay, define one for me?"

"Can we move on?"

"You started this."

"Okay, I'll admit it, can we still move on? I want to hear about you, about all these adventures everyone is jabbering about."

"To start with, were it not for you, I wouldn't be at this high school class reunion. This is my first reunion ever, and it happens to be our 50th. That said I'm glad you wanted to see me. My life has been a struggle, if anything, it still is. If I've learned anything about myself, it is that I'm a very flawed man. I've also discovered I'm an introvert, that I don't like people, don't like crowds, don't like belonging, but have a passion for ideas. I know I'm no genius, no more gifted than that guy building kitchen cabinets for rich folks' homes down in the valley.

"The difference between the next guy and me is that I pay attention to ideas. At the same time, and this may sound contradictory, I'm not overly impressed with the history of ideas. By the accident of my birth, I live in an age when people are more interested in success than in living. Does any of this surprise you?"

He got the wrinkle of a smile in the corner of his eyes and said with a quiet nod, *"No."*

"You wanted to be a giant. Well, you are one." He said nothing. *"I owe you. We haven't seen each other for years, but I love you, guy."*

His face turned ashen and then red. It was clear this made him uncomfortable. *"Hey,"* I said, *"I'm not going to jump your bones!"* Why is it that we heterosexual males cannot love our gender unselfconsciously? I loved the purity of his pursuit; his selfless success; and his generous sharing of his wealth. His greatest impact, though, as he didn't punish me with his power, never did, although he could, and therefore his power blossomed into influencing me. *"It's not that kind of love,"* I added.

"I know that he said," too quickly.

"The word 'love' made you uncomfortable," I continued not letting him off the hook.

He looked at me and said, *"Did it?"*

"Yes, it was written in scarlet letters on your forehead in invisible ink."

"All right Nathaniel Hawthorne."

"No, I'm serious. You're an open book."

"Maybe to you," then seriously, *"it's always been your special skill, hasn't it?"*

"What?"

"Reading people."

"Why do you say that?"

"You sit processing data and reading me. One day I'll be in one of your books, and I know I won't like it." Then, as if a concession, *"and won't do anything about it."*

"No, you're too nice a guy. Writers are not nice people. I qualify. They write about nakedness and they don't touch up the portraits."

"Is that what it's like to be a writer? For God's sake, tell me about how you became one. That's why I wanted to see you. I wanted to understand what my mother saw."

Journey to Self-Knowing

"You want honesty, I suppose?" He nodded. *"Well, take my da. Like you, I had to struggle with him all his abbreviated life. He died only 49. The navy sent me home on emergency leave from the Med when he was dying. Because I was a chemist by training, and a hospital corpsman in the navy, his doctor allowed me to administer morphine shots to him for pain as he requested them.*

"I bathed him and put ointment on his bedsores, changed his sheets, shaved him, and all the other things a nurse might do. As he shriveled from a 160-pound man to barely 60 pounds, as the disease ravished his body, inch by inch, pound by pound, day by day, reducing him to little more than a memory, we talked.

"Now, I thought, he will enlarge on what he first said to me before I went overseas. I asked him, 'Do you remember what you said to me when I left?'

"His yellowed eyes just stared. 'You said you were more worried about me than my brother and sisters, do you remember saying that?' He still just stared. 'You said I didn't even write a good letter and I'd starve to death as a writer, do you remember saying that?'

He blinked as if to say, no. *"You also said I thought I was so friggin smart and wasn't smart at all. Remember that? Said I was a dumb bastard if you asked him. Do you remember?"* He just shook his head weakly. *"Well,"* I continued, *"you did. I'm not saying you were wrong. I'd just like a bit of clarification is all."* He turned to me and asked for some water. After he drank it out of a straw, he smiled almost a wicked smile,

"Isn't Raw Hide on about now?" I nodded. *"Can we watch it?"* I nodded again. He got a morphine glow, waiting for me to turn on the TV.

"He had a little black and white nine-inch television, the first he had ever had. He loved the westerns such as Raw Hide and Wagon Train. His favorite on Raw Hide was Clint Eastwood, whom he said looked like me. I couldn't see the resemblance, so I asked what he saw in him.

'He's cocky like you, thinks his shit doesn't stink, doesn't like to take orders, and," I interrupted.

"But you said he looked like me, how do you mean?" I'll admit I was fishing for a compliment. Eastwood was tall and blond and so was I. "He's got asshole written all over his face," He offered with no rancor in his voice, "you can see that can't you Jimmy?" Wonderful.

"That told me I would have been better off to have left it alone. I knew then that death was not far away. He died more than 46 years ago. It has taken me that long to understand that he wasn't malicious. I was too dense and self-absorbed to pick up his meaning. So what does this have to do with my being a writer? Well, everything, and nothing, I guess. You decide.

"One day when I was writing a book about my early years in this town I came across something that stunned me. It shook me so badly that I heaved such heavy sobs that I thought I was going to pass out for the lack of oxygen to my brain. Describing it now may make little sense to you, but it knocked me on my ear then."

"Let me decide," my friend said, anxious for me to continue, "Just tell your story, don't worry about how I'm going to take it."

"Well, it was something he had written in lower case cursive on a government handout. The good Sisters of St. Francis weren't too successful in teaching him penmanship or spelling. Come to think of it the poet, e. e. cummings was celebrated for his lower case shenanigans.

"What turned my insides out was this government publication for the newly born: United States Department of Labor, Children's Bureau, Publication No. 8: Infant Care. It was a book he received after I was born, and was covered with his adoring scribble, I suppose, waiting to take my mother home from Mercy Hospital. "Then I found a small sign, obviously professionally printed, Welcome Home Mama & Jimmie Ray. It moved me.

"I know telling you this, it must sound histrionic. No big deal. I assure you, it was a shock to my system, a man wrote this who was excited when I was born but never excited about me again. He never came to *my games, never had anything to say about my grades, never saw me hold the highest honor of an altar boy at a Solemn High Mass celebrated by the Bishop of the Davenport Diocese, never saw me play baseball at Review Stadium as a boy with men twice my age, never said anything when I was elected Secretary of State at Hawkeye Boys' State, never congratulated me for making all-state honorable mention in football, or playing varsity basketball for four years, never said anything about my winning a Merit Academic Scholarship to the University of Iowa, never attended my graduation when I graduated from college cum laude Phi Beta Kappa.*

There I was, confronted with how he saw me as I came into the world, then nothing. When I had regained my composure, I reflected on what he had told me over a lifetime that I had conveniently forgotten but had internalized.

"He said they can take the clothes off your back, the roof over your head, the food off your table, the money in your pocket, but they have to kill you to take away what you put between your two ears.

"On another occasion, he said all any man needs to live is a place to throw his hat, a roof over his head, three square meals a day, and the rest is gravy. If you're into gravy, and measure who you are by how much gravy you have, you'll never stop running until you die because you'll never have enough.

"Then I thought of other things he said that my mother tried to soften the sting, such as 'you're the son of an Irish Roman Catholic brakeman on the railroad. That is who you are. The day you forget that you won't know who the hell you are.

"What amazed me is he never read anything but sometimes his admonitions had a distinct Greek sentiment: 'You want to fly high into that sun Jimmie, but I'll tell what, they're going to clip your wings the moment they see you're flying too high and mighty, and a threat to them, then you're going to fall so hard it could kill you. You're not one of them, never will be, they'll never accept you, sure they'll use you, but don't let that stir your shit too much, because as soon as they use you up you're gone. Never get too comfortable around them, Jimmie,

never drop your guard, or they'll find three ways to Sunday to destroy you, do you hear me, Jimmie?

"It always made him uncomfortable to see me reading. He saw it as a feminine inclination. Once he said, 'you have such a constipated brain I don't think there is an enema that could clean you out of all your shit.' Another time, 'all of us are little criminals, Jimmie, but I'll tell you one thing, poor people's sins are all venial, rich people's sins are all mortal sins, there's no way to get wealthy except dishonestly on the backs of the honest.'

"Of course I didn't hear him, then, but much of what he warned me about however came true."

During this long soliloquy, my college roommate of decades ago sat there with his sad eyes and said nothing. *"You are as I remember you, remarkably so, paranoid still, but the reader of people. I remember your memory. God, how I envied it! You don't seem to forget anything. Your father was right. You probably have a pretty constipated brain."*

I laughed. *"You think?"* Then continued, *"True, I take in everything and file it away to be used later, possibly in a book. I suppose writing is my enema. In any case, as my da was dying and taking his last breath,*

"I was filling my memory bank, taking in the room, the smells, the stillness, the darkness, the feeling of it all, the furnishings, the huge hospital bed in that little room, a bed loaned to us by the American Cancer Society, the "paid-in-full" handwritten note on the nightstand from Dr. Joseph O'Donnell who hadn't been paid a dime, the smudged doily crocheted by my mother on a little medicine table with a morphine syringe and bottle of camphor, the grief and relief on my mother's face as she moved her lips saying the Rosary silently, her refusal to believe him gone until I put a glass to his lips and there was no condensation, my inability to shed a tear, but to calculate how I could finesse the church from the Mass offerings and give it to my mother, the approach I would use on my da's Irish mortician friend to get a bargain basement price on a casket, the need yet to call on the railroad to determine my mother's benefits, the value of the house, and how much mortgage was

left, the best way to handle my one sister who was devoted to him and him to her, the mystical meaning of passing to the other side, and how I might use this, the emotional state of the family which was always an open wound.

"Would it heal now, or be a permanent sore? How could I escape from here with all this to face? It never occurred to me until much later what a hero he had been in a long, painful, and protracted illness without complaint or self-pity. I think the reason I couldn't cry, although I wasn't conscious of it at the time, was my disappointment that he was so much more courageous in death than he had ever been in life.

"What would remain most vivid would be the way his eyes in death locked on me, followed by a tremendous sigh, then the inevitable death rattle, and finally, as the soul left his body as if it could be seen, his face transfigured from pain to benevolent peace. He was now with the angels, and I was certain of it.

"My mother suddenly became hysterical as she wrapped herself around his body, and kept saying, 'Jimmie, is he all right, is he all right?' This was after I had proved him gone. I pulled her away and put her head on my shoulder, 'Mother, he's gone. He's at peace now. There's no more pain. He's with God now.' She started to cry, not hysterical tears, but moist sighs of honeydew like a child who has been forgiven a slight transgression.

"It was a perfect time to cry, to let go, and let all of this anxiety evaporate, but I couldn't. I was stoic, almost cold, analytical, and lost in what had to be done. My goal was to give him the funeral of a saint, simple, elegant, and sacred, and I did.

"It was in the succeeding weeks that I would run into his railroad cronies and find some liked him and some didn't. When they would describe his misgivings, I imagined them their own. He was not one to badmouth others or to relish in their misfortunes. He was generous and kind. At the same time, he was cocky and pugilistic and would fight at the drop of a hat. Physically, he never met a man who could bully him. 'Bullies, Jimmie,' he said, 'are afraid of their own shadow.' He

wasn't afraid of men; he wasn't afraid of death; he died like a saint. And like most saints, he was afraid of life.

"The unconscious is never a force that bubbles up to the surface too frequently, leastwise with cue cards and loud whispers as to the hidden meanings stirring below. It didn't for me then. What did happen is that I changed. I knew I wouldn't be a lab chemist anymore. I wouldn't sit there doing titrations and paper chromatographic analyses. I wouldn't sit in technical meetings and hear consultants chirp about what we already knew. I wouldn't spend hours in the research library studying competitors' patents to circumvent chemical processes and duplicate their proprietary products. I wouldn't remain in that cloistered world of envy, animosity, and small thinking, that world of big brains and little power. I would venture out into that world that so intimidated my da.

"But life sometimes plays tricks on you, doesn't it? The words I heard so many years ago from that uneducated brakeman rattled my cage. Success found me one day in South Africa forming a new company, a country with unfathomable beauty in people, topography, and culture. Yet, I wasn't prepared for apartheid, the policy of the separation of the races, a policy in which the white minority imposed draconian conditions on the black majority.

"Suddenly, the easy climb to the top of my little hill brought little satisfaction. Suddenly, I saw myself no different than the trapped Bantu tribesmen. I was shanty Irish, after all, not lace curtain, out of my depth. Suddenly, I saw the Afrikaner trapped as well in his policy of apartheid. Afrikaners were good people who had allowed ignorance and fear to drive them into this cage.

Then I saw my Church up close and personal, both in Rome and South Africa. It was a shock to me, to realize a tacit agreement existed between the government and the church to maintain the status quo. I identified with the Bantu. My da often spoke of how the British subjugated Northern Ireland. I identified with the Afrikaner or Boer, too, as I was from a farm state, and was used to being considered unsophisticated. Well, Afrikaners played into this bias.

"But I couldn't identify with my Church. My church had always been my anchor. I never questioned its authority. Now, my faith started to unravel, a faith that I thought was as solid as South African diamonds and sparkled with the same radiance.

"It was clear that in this game of life I had lost my momentum and needed to take a 'time out' and regroup. Once this was clear to me, good coach of myself that I was, I didn't hesitate to resign. Sure, there was flack. I moved my family to Florida from South Africa, and my boss came down to try to understand what was going on.

"You say I can read people. That's not true. Most people read others in terms of themselves. That was the case with my boss. He couldn't understand how I could give up so much when I was just getting on the 'gravy train.' So incredulous and persistent was he that I became blunt. If I weren't doing my job, I told him, you'd have grounds to fire me. Well, the company, no fault of its own, is not meeting my needs. I'm firing the company.

"It was that simple. He didn't believe me. For the next two years, some ways subtle others not, the company checked to see if I was selling company secrets or if I had gone rogue with a competitor. I was reading and writing, and playing a little tennis. That was it. When I was nearly broke, I went back to school full time for the next six years. Not what everyone would do, but what I had to do."

My friend's fists were clasped under his chin, his face pensive. *"Go on!"* he declared. *"That's not all of it, is it?"*

"No, I did write one book early on to explain this so-called ability to read people. It took me only six weeks, and it stayed in print for twenty years. It is my all-time best seller and I wrote it off the top of my head, which should tell me something, but unfortunately, it hasn't.

"What was it like going back to school after being out so many years?" he asked.

"I was coming to that but thought in all fairness that what I have to say may sound a little harsh. There is questing in me. I guess you could say I am searching for the real parents of my soul. I expected too much

from my church, failing to recognize that it is the most human institution that there is. The same could be said of the university. These are flawed institutions created by flawed men looking for answers, and only finding more flawed questions for the exercise.

"How could it be any different? The atoms of my brain were bouncing against my cranium as if in a cyclotron without splitting into revelation. I expected from the university the same thing I expected from my church, to do all my heavy lifting, and of course, that is neither their function nor competence.

"Labelers can call this the postmodern era, but nothing has escaped the factory mentality. Everything is packaged for disposable use, and I mean everything. That was hard for my mind to accept. Dropping out, as I did, would have offended my da, but he would have seen it consistent with how he saw me. A half lifetime ago, I abandoned my life as it was, and have been on this uncertain path ever since. I went on my way to find my way."

"Do you think you've found it? Have you realized closure?" My friend asked these questions with such emotion that I immediately understood there was another agenda for this meeting. He was looking for an Oracle. I'm sure I wasn't the first man he sought out for this role, and certainly, I wouldn't be the last.

"I hope this doesn't disappoint you," I confessed, "I haven't found my way because I'm still on it, and I now realize there is no such thing as closure."

All the life seemed to drain out of his face. He removed his glasses and polished the lenses. His eyes were red and moist, perhaps from the lights. He hastened for me to continue waving his handkerchief as he put his glasses back on.

"What I have learned and the reason I shared this story with you is that the hardest thing is to like ourselves. We hear a lot about self-love and how damaging it can be, but we never hear anything about liking ourselves as we are. Another word for liking ourselves is self-acceptance. This is not accepting ourselves as we should be, but as we

are, not as others choose to see us, but as we see ourselves, not in terms of arbitrary standards such as success and failure, but as our own best friend.

"I don't say this lightly. I think now of all the books I've read, studied, and devoured, books I've highlighted, written on the sides of the text, even kept logs and manuals of them for future reference. What I discovered is that in the end, I was still left with me. That each one of these people I read was writing about themselves. They were struggling with their questions, giving off a common echo, the echo of a person running from himself only to constantly run into himself ad infinitum, ever hoping that the last collision would not reoccur.

"I finally reached the point of recognizing all my sins, realizing all my little successes and failures were only tiny blips on my radar screen, knowing my passing would differ little with my da's.

"Each of us as we come to our journey's end must realize we come in alone and leave alone, and that the portrait we paint can be either Oscar Wilde's Dorian Gray or an honest reflection of a life well-lived.

"One day when I was consulting, I sat down at my desk and thought of an African American young man in the group who was talented but had an attitude. I wrote a short article that started with this line: To have a friend you must be a friend starting with yourself. It became a prize-winning article with tens of thousands of requests for reprints. It also became the seeds of The Taboo Against Being Your Own Best Friend.

"So that," I said, in surrender with my hands high above my head, *"is that! You now know something of this writer's cage."*

We rose together. He gave me a bear hug, and said, *"Thank you."* He didn't look back as he left the restaurant, his shoulders drooping in deep thought. We never spoke again during the weekend.

Time Out for Sanity! Blueprint for Dealing with an Anxious Age, 2nd Edition (2015) – Originally published as **"A Look Back to See Ahead"** (2007)

The author contends that early 21st century America mirrors the United States of Anxiety of the 1970s in many disturbing ways. He states simply that we are stuck in the decade of the 1970s with little sense of how to move on. Despite rhetoric to the contrary, everything changed after 1969, marking the early end of the American Century.

The United States watched its power fade and its markets shrink as old competitors in Europe and the Far East prospered with new competitors emerging, while the American nation's confidence and identity took a severe hit.

Dr. Fisher shines a bright light into this darkness revealing our collective complacency while claiming this status threatens to become nothing less than the norm. He sees people today as busy as ever, moving faster and faster while absurdly remaining essentially in place. It is the 1970s dressed up in 21st-century fashions failing to acknowledge the mindset is fixated on the past.

In the 1970s the escape from anxiety was on a psychedelic high with recreational drugs. Today it is an obsessional retreat of existence into common and pervasive electronic pacifiers in virtual reality.

The book asks the question: has society changed; have we changed; if so, why so; if not, why not?

Dr. Fisher sees American society going from Past Imperfect to Present Ridiculous when Future Perfect is a mythical destination that never occurs. All we ever have is the present, ridiculous or not.

The Information Age has exploded in our midst and we have lost our way, allowing Silicon Valley and its arbiters to dictate our future with the notion that science and technology will show us the way when they are part of the insanity. In any case, "Time Out for Sanity" revisits this problematic situation.

From the pages of "Time Out for Sanity!"

BACKGROUND REFERENCE:

During the Christmas holidays in 2006, rummaging through my accumulated archives of published and unpublished material, I came across this manuscript. It was written when I was fresh from my most recent stint in academia in the late 1970s, having received my Ph.D. It was a time of palpable madness as some readers may recall:

When young people were forced to participate in an unpopular war (VIETNAM); when political upheaval was in the air; when corrupt politicians lied and deceived the electorate; when this deception reached a crescendo with WATERGATE; when drugs were ruining lives; when morality took a holiday; when new forms of bigotry and hatred were being hatched; when the automotive industry was in sharp decline, while foreign automakers were eating our lunch; when an energy crisis rocked the land with OPEC's oil embargo; when a paranoid president (NIXON) hunkered down and became a law unto himself; when US CONGRESS stayed the same, missed the changes, wouldn't face them, and left the future up for grabs.

This essay incorporated themes I would eventually expand on in *"A Look Back to See Ahead"* (2007), however putting it on hold in 1978 and writing about other things.

"Is society sick?" was originally a ninety-page essay written more than forty years ago. As you read this work consider its themes in the context of today, asking yourself: has society moved towards healing, and if not, why not?"

Note: A version of this original essay appears on my blog (peripateticphilosopher.blogspot.com January 2006)

"IS SOCIETY SICK?" – As first written in 1978

"May we not be justified in reaching the diagnosis that, under the influence of cultural urges, some civilizations, or some epochs of civilization – possibly the whole of mankind –have become neurotic? We may expect that one day someone will venture to embark upon a pathology of cultural communities."

Sigmund Freud, *Civilization and Its Discontents* (1930)

We are taught from an early age not to think but to do; to accept formulated programming by society. This is reinforced in school and church and sustained by media. Natural skepticism is blunted by an incessant bombardment of a cultural point of view.

Consequently, the last person one cues on is oneself. The last authority one respects is that of one's authority. Many observers, among them Erich Fromm, Eric Hoffer, Pitirim Sorokin, R.D. Laing, and T. S. Szasz, echo the sentiments of the man-on-the-street.

The shift away from a community-centered society finds the individual on his own. The Renaissance spirit is disregarded in the lives and works of ordinary citizens. For that reason, these pathfinders appear strangely as *"societal misfits"* or outsiders.

They have dared to see and to be. It is time for correction; time to shed illusory and iconic images, and to endure the pain and surprise of a new dawn. If society is sick, it can only be saved one person at a time, a person not afraid to proclaim the emperor has on no clothes.

Authenticity is needed to come to grips with this plight. My pastor confesses to his parishioners, *"It is impossible to know whom to believe,"* a direct reference to disclosures of Watergate. *"I held out to the very last that the president would be exonerated, that the whole thing was a media fiasco."* He throws his sermon to the floor. *"Never again will I believe in any of them!"*

Melodramatic? Juvenile? He is not through. *"I should have been born in the twelfth century when sanity ruled."*

Of course, he is wrong but feels everyone listening is equally ignorant, mesmerized by his theological office. Sanity, if anything, has taken a holiday with a return to *"The Age of the Crusades and Inquisitions."*

What he should have said is that the twelfth century was an era of transition as is the present. Then he would have given his parishioners a perspective to consider in the light of current events. Society was sick not only because of that *Inquisition* but because of the monarchial authority and feudalistic zeal of the church to dominate and control ordinary souls in all phases of their existence.

To romanticize this period is to give short shrift to good sense. This happens when public trust is put on a pedestal to see people and events as more than human to treat them as less than human. When we fail to see humanity, as it is, evil as well as good, it makes a mockery of us all. Our cloying dependence on outside authority for internal security demonstrates how completely immature that young priest was in one sense, and how well he knew his parishioners in another.

He was shaped and molded, in part, by the media he despises. He has since left the church, cynical and disenchanted, still clinging to his illusions. He was not prepared to cope with Watergate, he says, but that is not quite the case. He managed to project and transfer his frustrations to this convenient scapegoat – as many of us have done – without gaining an iota of insight into Watergate or himself.

He epitomizes the person shaped by other men's minds without being introduced to his own. He represents a prototype of the times that uses events outside experience to justify self-indulgence.

Our society never mentions our secret desires, but they are behind every word. We live in a culture where the passivity of hope dominates. This leads to missed opportunities and wasted energy that we all know so well. In the end, chances are the reader decides the issue of sickness or wellness based on his or her perspective and experience, as it should be.

HAVE A LOVE AFFAIR WITH WHAT YOU DO!

"There are pauses amidst study, and even pauses of seeming idleness, in which a process goes on which may be likened to the digestion of food. In those seasons of repose, our powers are gathering their strength for new efforts; as land which lies fallow recovers itself for tillage."

American clergyman J. W. Alexander (1804 – 1859)

All of us must work, but we differ widely in our interpretation of that experience. We differ in our sense of role, duty, obligation, and responsibility. It is more likely that work happens to us rather than is created out of love. Since it is more likely something we have to do rather than want to do, it is doubtful that love is a consideration. We fall into work but not the way we fall into love. There is intense pleasure and anticipation when we fall into love. We take leave of our senses to rediscover them. Words such as fulfillment, completion, and wholeness only come to mind after the fact when we are one with our mate.

Why not the same with work? There is a simple answer. Love is a relationship. It is personal. It is intimate. It makes us more than we are. It is appreciative. We never tire of telling our mate how much we love him or her because it is more than we ever expected, more than we sense we deserve. Every moment of every day is a blessing.

Work, on the other hand, has been reduced to money. We measure success, status, clout, importance, and security in terms of money. Money is a thing without personality; with no chance of intimacy; no sense of satisfaction, which always makes us feel less than we are. It is a reward for doing something that we are paid to do, and therefore it is a material, not a spiritual connection.

Money becomes so important to us that even love is measured in terms of money. We would rather give our mate an expensive gift than our loving attention. Indeed, love has been reduced to commerce: *"Diamonds are a girl's best friend."* Diamonds are cold, hard, and inanimate and reflect brilliance without having any. They are love's substitute for the intimacy of a personal nature, which translates into spending quality time together. With money, we never have enough because someone always has more.

We compare and compete with others by having better homes, bigger cars, larger wardrobes, bigger bank accounts, and stock portfolios, always more. We never have enough. The axiom follows the less we enjoy work the more important is money. Money becomes an unconscious effort to punish our employer for making us do something we don't want to do but have talked ourselves into believing we have to do.

All of us fall across a spectrum of love and hate when it comes to working. No work is ever perfect, nor is any worker. Our approach to work differs according to our state of mind. We live in a material world, but we also live in a spiritual world. We live in a world of things, but also a world of people. If we have a job we love, and a mate that completes us, we are blessed with an angelic touch of heaven. We don't have to say a word to let the world know how we feel about work. It shows in our countenance, the way we move, clearly demonstrating whether work is a chore or a joy.

The disgruntled worker acts as if the world owes him a living when the employer owes him only a full day's pay for a full day's work and no more. The employer is not his keeper, not there to bail him out for his poor money management; not there to excuse his excesses; not there as an apologist to excuse the consequences of his actions. We are masters or slaves of our existence. What is there about those who seem always happy at work, who tackle each assignment with enthusiasm, and who embrace the challenge and ride disappointment with equal ease?

Better yet, who do they most resemble? The adult. Then why are there so few? Think of high achievers you know in any endeavor, who never tire of raising the bar and achieving at a higher level, then ask yourself why there are not more of them? We are all part of nature and grow once we seed our effort, and tend to grow consistent with nature's requirements.

But the ground must be fertile, the climate conducive, and the cultivation appropriate to the growing. Perhaps that is what is missing. It is no accident that some students work to learn while others work only for grades. The learner derives something new that is part of him or her for life. The grade grabber leaves learning behind clinging to credentials.

Work is love made visible when our outsides catch up with our insides for work is a measure of all things.

START CUING ON YOURSELF!

"The problem is that literate and civilized people do not understand that their brains are much smarter than their minds."

Alan W. Watts, British American Philosopher

The very last voice we hear, the very last place we look to for answers is ourselves. This is as true of the educated as to the uneducated, in fact even more so. The educated are programmed to conform and respond to the system. They cannot write a paper without access to references meant to give the paper credence when it only demonstrates the lack of imagination and originality.

We hold ourselves in the lowest of esteem when it comes down to the nitty-gritty. Infrequently, when our intuitive voice cuts through conformity, we make decisions consistent with ourselves. Otherwise, we look everywhere for answers but where they reside. Small wonder marriage counselors, psychic gurus, management consultants, psychotherapists, and clinical psychologists have a full calendar of obliging prospects to swallow their bromides as implicit wisdom.

Dr. Thomas Harris states that ninety percent of us see everyone else as "okay," but ourselves as "not okay." No matter what our situation, we never see ourselves as having either enough education or income to consider ourselves "okay."

Incredible as it may seem, we see ourselves as under-educated, under-skilled, and under-qualified to deal with our own lives. We think others are better able to address what is only salient to us. This doesn't throw us into action to right this deficiency. It throws us into a swoon of inertia. We believe the key to our destiny is in an authority figure unfamiliar with us as a person when we already have that key in our hands. We don't want to do something. We want someone to alleviate our angst. Many of us are like the man who is starving with a loaf of bread under his arm.

So terrified are we of events over which we have no control that we box ourselves in and then hand our fate over to someone else. Take the mother who watches the six o'clock news on television and is so overwhelmed she cannot make dinner or the father who hears rumors of the plant closing and cannot get out of bed to go to work. In both instances, mother and father are living on the edge abdicating their harmony and equilibrium to a foreign voice, a proposition carried to the extreme.

Consequently, the last person we trust is ourselves; the last person we have confidence in is ourselves; the last person we gamble on is ourselves, and the last person we invest in is ourselves. We will invest in a house to shelter us and as a hedge against inflation. We will invest in an automobile to carry us from here to there. We will invest in nice clothes to make the correct impression on people who count. But we will feel guilty if we seek education with no apparent instrumental justification.

We see people reading books that have nothing to do with work and sense that they are idlers, but we think nothing of those spending happy hours after work in local pubs. They are unwinding.

The cultivation of the mind for its enjoyment is best kept a secret to avoid ridicule, but it needn't be. Few see it as a waste to gamble over which we have no control: stock market, athletic contests, and the lottery. The essence of gambling is that the stakes are loaded against us. Even if we win, it is not earned. What is not earned is not appreciated. Then too, it is avoiding the struggle, which is life, where only what we earn is ever valued. It is well to remember that the inner voice tells us not only where we are going, but also why we are going there. To hear it we must cue in on ourselves.

SO, YOU HAVE *ROCKS IN YOUR HEAD*! WELCOME TO THE CLUB!

"The great breakthrough in the contemporary theory of mental illness is that it represents a kind of stupidity, a limitation or obtuseness of perception, a failure to see the world as it is. It is not a disease in the medical sense, but a failure to assign correct priorities to the real world."

Ernest Becker, *Revolution in Psychiatry* (1964)

To be human is to be mysterious and mystifying. There is not a man alive without secrets, deep and dark secrets that he fears would be his undoing if they "got out." Nor is there a man alive without perverted ways. We tend to see such ways only in sexual terms, but that is only the tip of the iceberg. There are far more damaging perversions in society notwithstanding myths to the contrary.

Morality is in the mind of the time. Morality is itself a perversion. It is constructed of taboos and perverted myths that poison the soul from generation to generation. *The Inquisition* and *witch-hunts* come to mind. Monstrous perversions have been done in the name of religion that today would quake the immortal soul. Depravity yesterday is common practice today.

We create a private hell for ourselves by buying into what society sanctions in its ambivalence. The decadence of the 1920s, the *Flapper Era,* when young people reportedly "went wild," would be considered mild fare today.

People of the *Great Gatsby* ilk line both coastlines in conspicuous ostentation, while being celebrated as leading citizens. Then some cue on self-righteous themes amid hedonism. Many have been "born again." In surrendering to a new austerity, they forget why wine, women, and song consume a time.

People depart from moral restriction for reason. Society finds it necessary to break from stultifying rectitude to breathe, when transitioning from one form of society to another that results in spinning off in a maddening dash to new meanings.

People have little sense of why such diversions from the previous norm surface. They see excess as sin, which is meaningless when waste is the culprit. The lack of limits is the sin of our times and why society is in the throes of a nervous breakdown.

When everyone behaves the same when leadership mimics this sameness, society is adrift and no one is in charge. We are in a decade of confused leadership where authority has no meaning at any level: home, school, church, work, or government. This is largely because those in authority attempt to hide their weakness: that is, parents, teachers, priests, bosses, and politicians.

Great leaders are plagued by great weakness. Lincoln suffered depression and melancholy most of his life; Churchill was an alcoholic and suffered depression. Hitler and Napoleon behaved civilly in their personal life, neither smoking nor drinking, but barbarically in their military ambitions. Hitler was extremely careful in his diet with a regiment of proper sleep and exercise. Neither Lincoln nor Churchill worked regular hours pushing themselves often beyond their limits.

What these leaders held in common was an awareness of their historic significance, careful to manage their image away from their human failings. Only Hitler failed to see the humor in his limitations while the others shared theirs if obliquely.

Why is a man unable to tolerate what he is not? Why is it so hard for him to see the natural connection between strength and weakness, the bond between good and evil that exists in us all? Why the ambiguity of madness, as if madness is a rarity when madness is as common to the human spirit as is sanity?

It is madness that sparks creativity. It took madness to create the great symphonies, paintings, literature, and architecture. Madness escapes the norm. How could Milton create *"Paradise Lost,"* or Dante *"The Divine Comedy"* without an acquaintance with madness?

Creativity is not rare but common. Alas, it is killed in many of us before it catches hold. The instinct for self-preservation and approval clashes with the impulse for internal widening and spiritual awakening. Outsiders have penetrated these barriers and have built the society we know by focusing on themselves as individuals at great sacrifice. They are change agents standing for truth that Colin Wilson suggests in *"The Outsider"* (1956) *begin as outsiders and finish as saints.*

It is impossible to grow as an individual unless strength is understood in terms of weakness, goodness in terms of evil instincts, energetic commitment in terms of laziness, and sanity in terms of its twin, madness.

Since madness is where creativity lies, it must be employed for sanity to triumph. *The growth of a man* is an orchestration of self-acceptance complemented by the acceptance of others as they are found. The only person you can change is yourself, no other. Without that understanding, there is no growth, only parody. These secrets are part of your essence. To tap them only takes their acknowledgment.

CELEBRATE YOUR ADVERSITY!

"A smooth sea never made a skillful mariner, neither do uninterrupted prosperity and success qualify for usefulness and happiness. The storms of adversity, like those of the ocean, rouse the faculties and excite the invention, prudence, and skill, and fortitude of the voyager. The martyrs of ancient times, in bracing their minds to outward calamities, acquired a loftiness of purpose and a moral heroism worth a lifetime of softness and security."

Anonymous

The most common story told with each success is devoid of the more compelling story, which is its brother, failure.

Failure is a precious gift of an experience that no one can give to another no matter how much love they hold for that person. Failure is the scent of the wine's bouquet before its taste passes the pallid. The scent precedes the taste of success; its essence is its bouquet. Failure is an expression of having the mettle to try with no chance of being held up by someone else should failure come. There is little appreciation of success unless it is preceded by failure.

Fermentation gives a wine its bouquet; failure gives success its essence. There is no substitute for the fermentation of experience. Nor is there any chance of growth without pain. Information can be acquired, precaution can be taken, but the progression from inadequate to adequate to proficient involves pain and risk, and failure. The struggle is therefore not something to avoid but something to embrace. The greatest learning experience is limited to situations that might otherwise be described as risky or ill-advised. That is not to say one should court adversity at the expense of good fortune. It means simply that adversity is likely to touch everyone's life in the course of living and should not cripple one, or cause one to view life as hopeless when it occurs.

Genius is the name of persistence. Adversity has many faces. One man's adversity may be another man's good fortune. It is all in the mind of the beholder. One takes his bumps in the road and chalks them up to experience; someone else is traumatized by the bumps and looks for a less demanding course. Good fortune comes to those who take all shades of trouble in stride as part of the cycle of failure and success to be encountered in that quest.

Think back over your life and reflect on your successes and failures and ask yourself this question: what did I learn and when did I learn it?

Frequently, what happens when we are enjoying success is that we don't think at all. If we do think, we wonder when the other shoe will fall, and failure will return. Failure is always the ghost in the wing taunting us off stage. It stands to reason a string of good fortune must be followed with failure, right?

No one can always be successful, but yet some people are. Why is that? Could it be that they constantly review the lessons learned in failure, and reapply them to success? We wonder in this odd way when we are failing but not when we are succeeding. It is apt to find us uptight when the best of all worlds are visiting us, strange as it may seem. We fear the worse and everyone's face is its reflection, and so the caution.

Then there is the possibility we cover ourselves in martyrdom's garb when we are failing to lick our wounds and scorn others who refuse to lick them for us. As natural as failure is to our development, and as important as it is in building our character, failure is misunderstood.

It is a failure, or adversity that wakes us out of our doldrums, kicks us into action as our instincts come into play. We have little awareness of our capacity to survive until motivated to prevail. Odd as it may seem, some fold up their tent, retreat into themselves and wait to be rescued. They ignore their strengths and play on their weakness.

This is not to say that retreat is always a bad strategy. There are times when it is the best strategy, such times as when the heart and mind need a respite of healing before moving on. Depression often takes hold when the mind is overwhelmed and the body is racked with a debilitating illness. We treat depression as a disease with drugs and talking cures, and even electric shock, God help us for that, yet depression pivots on the constant war between fight and flight. Discretion is the better part of valor when we take flight and recognize it is time to take a "time out."

The mind can only process so much information. When that information doubles, our capacity to cope is strained to the breaking point, and all kinds of alarm signals are going off telling us to slow down or even stop. We ignore them at our peril. The major reason we have wars between people is to escape the constant war within.

We project the object of our wrath on someone or something that reminds us of our horror. In our desperation to escape such confinement, we declare war on someone else. War is never rationale. War is always about hidden shame. It is the conflict generated by doing something even if it is wrong versus the inertia of doing nothing that plagues the spirit when dominated by the insanity of action.

Failure and adversity see through the con to what is hidden behind, which is the reality of experience. Einstein failed many examinations until he finally passed the one marked "truth." Edison and Tesla failed many times before they tasted success in the world of electricity. Failure is a great teaching tool. Failure is not merely a "trial and error" methodology. It is an exercise in persistence and a matter of retrial and correction.

A popular example is that of *Colonel Sanders* and the *"Kentucky Fried Chicken"* franchise. The colonel was sixty-five when an interstate highway cut right through the location of his restaurant. He had every reason to give up, retire, and go peacefully into the sunset. Instead, he took his recipe on the road in an attempt to sell it to restaurants. He had hundreds of rejections until he found success in a little restaurant in Utah. The rest is history. He lived to be a wealthy octogenarian, active and happy to the end. His wealth could not be measured in dollars for it was priceless.

IS IT SERIOUS?

Shakespeare's *Macbeth*

Look at all the long frowning and sad faces that greet you coming and going every day. Is your face one of them? What is it that matters to you? Is it your money? Your car? Your house? Your family? Your girl or boyfriend? Your wife or husband? Your children? Your education? Your career? The questions are endless.

What is it that life is all about anyway? Is it fame and fortune, pleasure and comfort, security and a worry-free existence? It is a fair question. I'm wagering you don't have the foggiest idea because there are no definitive answers. At best, our answers would be subjective and ambiguous. We worry about what has not yet happened, and probably won't because anxiety has become the luxury of a people with too much, too many, and too soon.

This is the sum and substance of life for whether you take it in stride or stridently, life goes on. Thank you very much. Worry surfaces when toys become more important than tools and distraction more appealing than attention.

Why is it we develop personal space and then fortify it with all sorts of disposable things, and then compound this insulation closeting ourselves in fenced-in communities? Is it our fear of others and life that we hide from the display? Or is it because we are ill-humored, lonely, shy, and afraid to venture beyond ourselves? *Nothing is private and therefore no one is.*

We gave that all up when we became an industrial society. Community is now an anachronism. Have you taken inventory of your priorities? Have you checked your mind for its grand design? Some people plan as if they intend to live forever, putting off living until they retire only to find they have run out of energy as well as time.

Why are we afraid? What do we fear? One of the most common fears is getting up in front of an audience and making a speech. Why is that? What do we want to protect? Our name? Our profession? Our reputation? Are we embarrassed for looking like a fool? We think speakers are different than we are when they are the same only with a sense of humor about the folly of exposure. So-called thinkers are no surer of themselves than the rest of us. They express their ideas to hear them outside themselves to calibrate the affirmation of the echo.

We do the same thing as talkers to our friends. For that matter, what is a thinker? Granted, some thinkers take themselves seriously, but that is because of arrogance. They truly believe they have answers to everything and for everyone. It is why smart people fail. They are so enamored of the purity of their thinking they lack an appreciation of its limitations. Consequently, they eventually make horrible blunders and come crashing down into humiliating disgrace.

There is no thinker, only conditioned thinking. The thought is conditioned. The mind is the storehouse of experience. Memory itself arises from conditioned thought. So, whoever the thinker, deep or superficial, the movement of the mind in any direction encounters its limits.

When the mind makes an effort to transform itself, it merely builds another pattern on top of the old. It is an effort of the mind to free itself from itself while only giving rise to a continuance of thought. It may be at a higher level but it remains in its sphere framed in that circle of thought and time. It is why more than one mind on a problem is prudence personified.

Is the world situation all that serious? Is the state of the economy all that serious? Is the state of your health all that serious? If you say, "yes" to these questions, then you are part of the collective con. I have heard these questions repeated all my life with circumstances whether than actions controlling the agenda, and always circling back on the same serious concerns.

The paralysis of analysis finds thinkers, whoever they are, failing to get beyond the barrier of conventional wisdom to meaningful action. That is why the problems solved are the problems thinking creates, *ad infinitum*. In one breath, we mouth, "This is serious," and in the other, "not my problem."

We fail to read the newspaper because it depresses us. We don't vote because *"all politicians are crooked, and it doesn't matter anyway."* We wish we could give up cigarettes, but say, *"we've got to die from something. Why not something that gives us pleasure?"* We think we take life seriously but we don't take it seriously at all.

What has happened to our inner fortitude? Are we traumatized by what is real and should be taken seriously, while fooled by what is not and beyond the pale of our consciousness? The evidence of this dilemma is that we wax serious when we don't give a damn, as fools fooling themselves. If so, who is the ultimate loser in this game if not us? The evidence is all around us.

After a century of "progress," we are leaving our planet a wasteland to be cleansed by some future global miraculous strategy. Does seriousness produce anything worthwhile? Are we happier or healthier, wiser or wealthier for being addicted to the rhetoric of progress? Where does this seriousness fit into a life plan where there are only remote and ambiguous sacrifices? These are questions only the reader can answer from the cast of characters in the gallery of his life.

LIFE IS A JOURNEY, NOT AN END, SO ENJOY!

"Following another is merely an effect of a deeper cause, and without understanding that cause, whether one outwardly follows or not has very little meaning. The desire to arrive, to reach the other shore, is the

beginning of our human search. We crave success, permanency, comfort, love, and an enduring state of peace, and unless the mind is free of this desire, there must be following indirect or devious ways. Following is merely a symptom of a deep longing for security."

J. Krishnamurti, *Commentaries on Living: Third Series* (1960)

"Nothing so much convinces me of the boundlessness of the human mind as its operation in dreaming."

William Benton Clulow (1802 – 1882) English Clergyman

What are you thinking at this moment? Ideas fly up from the page and set off little explosions in the mind, chasing you here and there, from this to that, to what and when as if you are on a magic carpet.

The mind is processing the words read to your unique kingdom of experience. In a way, you are in the embrace of the dream, which transports you, to another place. The dreamer in you has been released from its prison of doubt and conformity to speculate in the stillness of the mind where there is no interfering force. There is only stillness. There is no beginning, middle, or end. Your mind and this stillness are one. You are outside of time.

There is no before, now, or after. There is only "what is." Art and science have no business in your dream. There is no desire to analyze, no need to shade and select. There is no pain or pleasure, happiness or sadness. There is no construction of reality. There is no payoff for dreaming has no design or product, no need for cleverness or strategy, no need for symbols or processes, and most apparent of all, no need for continuity.

The dreamer goes where he wills governed by no strictures of logic. We are more than ourselves in our sleep for the slumber wakes up our souls. The experience, something that man has enjoyed since the dawn of consciousness, has come to have many names, but our dream has only one name, joy.

We like to call this stillness transcendental or meditation for it is beyond time and classification, a bit of heaven while we are still alive.

The release of the mind from its confinement regenerates the individual so that dividends accrue without effort, pain, or conscious thought. In the course of dreaming, the imagination crystallizes into imagery, which is revealed in fragments after the fact.

It is as futile to control the content of a dream as it would be to capture love in a bottle. Scientists declare dreaming as REM (rapid eye movement) or fitful sleep. Yet, we cannot be fully awake unless we have truly dreamed. We cannot fathom the world if we have not first dreamt it. Everything must stop before it starts, and that stopping is the stillness of the mind in the luxury of the dream. You cannot convince yourself that you are alert if you have never been otherwise. You cannot enjoy the moment if you are never in it fully. This is counterintuitive, but that is because we understand everything in terms of effort and there is no effort in the dream, no past, or fear of the future.

We have sacrificed the dream for dread and live in the consequence of that decision. All the symbols and concepts and ideas drilled into our heads in school do not constitute thinking. They constitute knowledge, and knowledge is not wisdom.

Understanding the simple is the meter of wisdom, and the simple first comes to us in our dreams. That is why we often solve complex problems in our sleep. Cutaway all the posturing and complexity, and we discover life in reflection is a process, not a product, a journey, not an end, a dream and not a plan, a joy and not a chore.

Dreaming is a force when the brilliance of the dream is never allowed to fade, as the future opens to us. Education is a process not to open doors or fill our pockets with gold, but to open our minds to the dream that lies dormant within us waiting to be released. Intelligence is the connection of the mind with the dream so that we live in the real and surreal world without anguish or apology as complements to each other.

Postponing joy is to miss the point. Joy is not something to bank on but something to be. Life is not an endurance contest meant to cope in misery. No one should be in a job or a career or a marriage that kills the spirit and thus the joy. Joy is the dream materialized. If the dream is dead and there is no place for joy, it is likely because the focus is on tomorrow, and what might be.

Misery joins self-pity in a mournful embrace. Yet, life can be a creative journey filled with joy instead of sorrow and stridency. True, few of us can capture our dreams in our waking hours as Dante and Milton did theirs, but we can determine to make choices that keep our imaginations alive.

YOU MUST DISBELIEVE BEFORE YOU CAN BELIEVE!

"We feel we cannot act without belief, because it is a belief that gives us something to live for, to work for. To most of us, life has no meaning but that which belief gives it; belief has greater significance than life. We think that life must be lived in the pattern of belief; for without a pattern of some kind, how can there be action? So our action is based on an idea, or is the outcome of an idea; and action, then, is not as important as the idea."

J. Krishnamurti, *Commentaries on Living: First Series* (1956)

Belief is blindness of culture. Since we are all products of our culture, we share in this blindness. Belief is a stop sign telling the mind to turn off because "we have arrived." The problem with this is that someone else is defining our destiny and the nature of our arrival. When you force the mind to believe what it cannot believe, its obedience is a lie. To have a culture that insists on beliefs that are no longer relevant or realistic is to give substance to the lie.

The weight of that culture is directed at self-preservation rather than challenging its beliefs. We live in such a culture. Fear is held over our heads if we confess doubt to such beliefs. This fear is compounded when a web of deceit and chicanery smothers doubters into silence.

When there is no room for doubt, when the collective will impinges on individual choice, then imagination, creativity, growth, and development are squeezed through a psychological strainer. The output is often the stench of rotting belief.

During this mind blindness, true believers carry the day, the herd mentality seeks comfort and advantage in the bosom of the popular norm. Clichés and stereotypes rule. True believers are cynical. They think everyone has an angle and is out to get as much as they can while the getting is good. They lack identity beyond the group, which explains the attraction.

As true believers, they have a cause to compensate for self-hatred. The words they use resonate with like-minded souls, yet they are always prepared to abandon the cause should it go out of favor. The attraction of true believers is to belong to something bigger than themselves, the envy of others, where special privileges and compensations accrue.

Each of us is blessed with the powerful filter of natural skepticism, which is far removed from cynicism. Skepticism prevents us from being taken in with what makes no sense to us, or which is not consistent with what we are and have experienced. It is a protective mechanism of the body and soul. We are limited to how our minds operate and process belief. It is well for us to disbelieve everything and anything before we entertain the possibility of belief.

This is because the mind can operate only with its projections, that is, with the things that are of its self. The mind has no relationship to the things that are not of their origin. It cannot process what it cannot fathom in the realm of what it has already experienced or contemplated or reasoned out before.

The trick used on the mind is that a word or symbol or phrase or emotionally laden disclosure touches a theme buried in our unconscious. All of us want approval. All of us want to belong. All of us want to be accepted. These basic needs can be exploited if our skepticism filter is not reinforced with self-identity, self-approval, and self-acceptance.

If not, then the mind can be cultivated and carried away with the bombast of someone else's agenda. That is why the promise of something for nothing, success without struggle, wealth without risk, or other clarion calls of similar nonsense should not dissuade us from our tasks. Don't ever apologize for being skeptical. It means you are in good health.

A TIME OUT IS GOOD FOR THE SOUL!

"Everything comes if a man will only wait."

Tancred Norman Crusader (1078 –1112)

If this essay does nothing more than cause you to pause and reflect, it has accomplished its aim. Life is very short, and as a friend recently reminded me: *"We hiccup, and a day, a week, a month, a year has gone by, making it even shorter than we think."* So enjoy every moment. And you will always be well.

Dr. James R. Fisher, Jr.
Second Edition
Time Out
For Sanity!
Blueprint for Dealing with an Anxious Age

Corporate Sin: Leaderless Leadership & Dissonant Workers, 2nd Edition (2016) – Originally published in 2000.

Author Fisher puts corporate society under analysis and sees its leaderless leadership unwittingly spawning dissonant workers to be the Corporate Sin of our times. It is now more important to impress than perform; to fit in than challenge the status quo; to concede to dysfunction than to confront such practices. In this matrix of conformity, there is no place for polite disagreement much less rebellion that ultimately sponsors growth and development in a climate of confrontation, managed conflict, and operational freedom.

An organization with no place for confrontation, Fisher insists, suspends the majority of the workers, who are now mainly professionals, in terminal adolescence as if still obedient twelve-year-olds in forty and fifty-year-old bodies.

While the corporate organization is not a healthy entity, Fisher argues something is filling the power breach as if by osmosis, promising a more suitable relationship between managers and these professionals. It is a paradigm shift so quiet that no one seems to notice. Work is moving away from the muscular masculine paradigm and toward the more subtle and less self-conscious feminine paradigm. Dr. Fisher sees this new paradigm shift resulting in workers using both sides of their brains as a palliative to the angst that previously had separated managers from workers and men from women in the business of the enterprise. Corporate Sin is a commentary designed to show how this is possible.

Corporate Sin

Leaderless Leadership and Dissonant Workers

James R. Fisher, Jr.

Something Is Wrong!

We all feel it. There is something fundamentally wrong in the workplace, wrong between workers and management. Mainly, despite lofty expectations, the new and growing majority class of workers has failed to achieve lift-off. As a whole, professional workers have failed to assert themselves with conviction. Sadly, this enormously capable segment of the workforce seems content to linger in the bosom of comfort; more concerned with protecting positions, than forging careers; more focused on the reaping than the sowing, more fascinated with the present than excited about the future.

Frustratingly, professionals have shown little inclination to self-manage. They do complain, however, and often with reason, but seldom with any purpose in mind, seldom with conviction. Instead, professionals have shown they highly esteem the traditional hierarchies of corporations, being obsessed with surmounting the corporate gauntlet for the promise of power and prestige.

What they fail to see, however, is that these relics of position power are about to vanish. Traditional management methods and structures, although pervasive, are now obsolete. In the context of a professional workforce, industrial age management techniques are old technology. Unfortunately, when professionals aspire to be managers, they abandon their province of expertise and enter a realm where the essential tools and methods of their discipline, their craft, are superfluous and potentially a handicap.

Assigning Blame

We could throw the blame on managers for creating this problem; management methods specifically, and we would be right; partly right that is. And, most people would not argue. But that would be letting professional workers off the hook. We would be saying, in essence, that professional workers are allowed to forego personal and professional obligations the moment they become employees. That is, each day as he or she walks through the office door to work, miraculously, a professional worker transforms from a responsible adult to an obedient child. We cannot, in conscience, condone such a deliberate renunciation of obligation.

Where Professionals Go Wrong

As the management track dissolves into a phantom ladder, managers continue to be paid more than professionals. This unsettles professional workers, who seem not to know what to do about it. So, they wait, indefinitely, to be rescued by a miraculous paradigm shift at no cost to themselves. The result:

Personality becomes a mere selling device. Friendship becomes a contact. The urge to improve deteriorates to mere acquisitiveness.

The function of work has changed, yet the structures around work remain the same. Inevitably, seeds of dissatisfaction are sown, provoking frustration. Like a crippled giant unable to walk, legions of professionals seemingly cannot find their legs. They possess the necessary skills, but not the courage to become self-directed, to stand on their own two feet. They are a product of outmoded human programming and they remain externally directed rather than self-directed, passive rather than engaged. Pathetically, they look to others for the solutions they alone possess. The new reality is that professionals must strive, are expected to enhance their talents and their places of work.

In tandem, companies struggle in a state of insecurity, wandering in a new wilderness. In business, there are no guarantees anymore, if there ever were. Nevertheless, certainties are still sought and expected, while the sustaining rhetoric persists. This merely adds to the confusion.

The Delicate Balance of Purposeful Work

We are a corporatist society and, accordingly, the waste of human capital and individual talent, in total, is a grave *corporate sin*. It is the reason for this book. Corporations, on the whole, do not understand how to leverage or develop their people, to maximize human potential and thus maximize their own. What is required is nothing less than a revolution; creative, courageous, leaders acting as architects of healthy, supportive work cultures. At the outset, corporate leaders, managers, and directors must:

(1) Reject the notion that there is a single ideal corporate workplace culture. Suspend the outside search for the model workplace culture. It doesn't exist;

(2) Devote energy and talents to the business of creating a beneficial work culture;

(3) Accept that the impetus for change invariably comes from the trenches, not from the mahogany row. People on the front lines have less to lose, and therefore are eager for change;

(4) Realize that people near the top, corporate executives, feel they have everything to lose by surrendering the status quo;

(5) Appreciate that we are in the midst of a quiet revolution, in which not only the color of workers' collars is changing, but also the complexion of the individual and collective will;

(6) Understand the key to purposeful performance is a Culture of Contribution; adults, not obedient children directing the activities of work; their work;

(7) View the pursuit of the optimal work environment as a work in progress characterized by ongoing change, experimentation, and adaptation; not a remedial program or fixed goal;

(8) Admit that management fumbled the ball by vigorously defending the status quo and business as usual practices, disconnecting from reality and respectful engagement.

Although disturbances representing the need for systemic change naturally bubble up from the bottom, the professed architects of change invariably emerge at the top. Since gridlock and stalemate are the bitter fruit of top-down change initiatives, *Corporate Sin,* the wasting of professional talent, continues unabated.

Historical Context

When the twentieth century dawned, ninety percent of workers were employed in agriculture. The working guilds of craftsmen and artisans were still very much in place. Work was primarily in small groups with no hierarchy, position power, or remote authority. Hand tools were used to make finished products. The collaborative corporate model was not yet in evidence. Job descriptions and role identity had to await the arrival of social engineers to create the nomenclature.

The Industrial Revolution was about to take off with rail, plane, and ship transportation connecting markets near and far. The world was exploding with new inventions among which were the radio, the telephone, the airplane, and motion picture, the automobile, and the electric power plant. Industrial centers were hastily created in urban areas hungry for bodies to run their factories causing a rapid shift of workers from the farm to the city.

In 1914, World War I broke out in Europe. This fueled a new iteration of technological development. The Panama Canal was finished and opened. Robert Goddard successfully launched a liquid oxygen and gasoline rocket. Weapons of war became more sophisticated with German submarines and Allied attack planes and battleships. Sir Arthur Stanley Eddington founded theoretical astrophysics. David Wark Griffith turned motion pictures from a curiosity into a viable new industry with "The Birth of a Nation." Alexander Graham Bell developed instant communications, making the first transcontinental telephone call from New York City to San Francisco to Dr. Thomas A. Watson with the message, "Mr. Watson, are you there?"

Education was changing, too, with the new curriculum ideas of John Dewey. He encouraged students to be independent thinkers and problem-solvers rather than rote learners. Albert Einstein published his theory of relativity. Even food preparation was changing. Clarence Birdseye invented the freezing and packaging of fresh foods, and called the products, "Birds Eye." Farming was changing as well with the gasoline-powered tractor replacing the oxen-driven plow.

In the wake of the "Great War," the war meant to end all wars, inconceivable prosperity turned into reckless indulgence against a backdrop of pervasive cynicism. Artists and writers, portraying themselves as members of the "Lost Generation," proclaimed the death of culture while flappers and their beaus embraced the "Roaring Twenties," dancing the Charleston all night to a Jazz Age beat. That is, until the party ended in 1929 with the stock market crash on Wall

Street, reverberating around the world, and triggering the Great Depression.

Against this backdrop, a new business class was emerging. Small guilds of tool and die, makers, fixture manufacturers, machine shop operators, and electrical component makers were merging into larger enterprises. They spawned corporations such as General Motors, Ford Motor, General Electric, Western Electric, Westinghouse, and American Telephone & Telegraph. These companies were financed with common stock issued to private investors who became absentee owners with no direct connection to company operations. Enter the *management class*.

Few former guild operators would emerge in control of operations as Henry Ford and Thomas Edison did. Managers were hired to oversee operations and boards of directors were created to set company policies. Workers were introduced to a new concept of repetitive "piece work." This would turn into the assembly line of mass production refined by Henry Ford in the manufacture of his Model T and Model A Ford.

Once wealth creators such as John D. Rockefeller, Andrew Carnegie, Henry Ford, and Thomas Edison stepped away from daily operations, executives in management roles, often members of the family, replaced them. These executives were employees, the same as all workers, family members or not, but quickly gravitated to the psychological identity of owners. To be fair, this was true to a point as part of executive compensation was in company stock. In contrast to this mentality, although 80 percent of employees are likely to own company stock today, few think of themselves as owners.

With the worldwide Great Depression of the 1930s, everyone suffered from the economic collapse, but none more than the poor. They had been forced into cities to work in factories isolating them from the land. Now, they were without jobs, no longer having farm properties to call home. Millions wandered the country with their families looking for work. John Steinbeck captures their plight in *The Grapes of Wrath*

(1939), a powerful indictment of capitalistic society highlighting the dangerous chasm between the rich and the poor.

Even employed workers were likely to live in hovels in city slums. Children as young as eight worked alongside adults in factories. Working conditions were horrific. Serious accidents and even deaths on the job were common. Workers had no medical benefits, unemployment compensation, or recourse to sue their employers. They were the working poor, the underclass, and came to see themselves as society's victims.

Labor unions evolved with workers participating in walkouts and manning picket lines. A terrifying period followed. During the 1930s, confrontations between thugs hired to protect company interests clashed with union workers to blacken society. This led to much bloodshed, which is hidden in the footnotes of history books.

The growing interdependence of the nations of the world was apparent as economic chaos swept the globe. The resulting societal turbulence proved fertile soil for the rooting of fascism in Germany and the rise to power of Adolf Hitler in 1933. The 1930s ended with Germany invading Poland. History's greatest conflict was set to begin like World War II. It was not America's war until a surprise attack.

On December 7, 1941, the naval and air forces of the *Empire of Japan* launched a surprise attack on the *United States at Pearl Harbor in Honolulu*. Four battleships were sunk including Arizona, four more disabled, eleven other ships were sunk, 188 aircraft were destroyed on the ground, and 2,330 servicemen and women and 100 civilians were killed. A slumbering giant became aroused.

The combination of America's manpower, management acumen, technology, natural resources, economic wealth, and common commitment would produce tanks, planes, ships, and weapons faster and in greater volume than all the Allies and Axis Powers combined. It was America's and American management's finest hour.

Hence, World War II established the management class, as we know it today. It took pride in the critical role it played in the war, and now it felt a license to exercise its muscle.

Management gurus surfaced dispensing corporate blueprints that defined the corporation as an entity housed in a central authority dispatching directives to divisions spread across the land to submit to corporate policies to the letter.

This rational ordering model treated workers as things to be managed, functions, not people to be led. This model was exceedingly successful during and immediately following World War II. Management possessed position power and hierarchical authority controlling recruiting, hiring, promoting, and firing with few if any challenges.

A set of standardized management tools followed, designed to maintain this control and efficiency. They were the following:

(1) Management by Objectives (MBOs)

(2) Strategic Planning

(3) Performance Appraisal

Management by Objectives (MBOs) was a process of dividing and subdividing objectives among departments and divisions until every operation had a slice of the same objective pie. Collating the results followed, and voila! We met our goal! Not quite.

MBOs worked much better on paper than in purposeful performance. It didn't matter. It was a ritualistic exercise that gave managers a sense of being involved sharing in the big picture. Besides, business was good to great.

Strategic planning, another time-consuming ritualistic practice, often proved wide of the mark, but mid-course corrections were what luxury management took for granted.

Performance Appraisal was the third staple in this toolkit, a process meant to enhance performance through continuous development.

Unfortunately, it drifted off that track to be a conference on salaries and merit pay.

MBOs, strategic planning, and performance appraisals were solid control mechanisms as long as people behaved as manageable profit-making centers and not as persons to be led.

Everything changed in 1970. It was then that the Vietnam War hit the consciousness of young people, who in mass rejected the war, as well as the managed society that sponsored and orchestrated it.

This disenfranchised segment of society stopped that war. Nothing has ever been the same since. Management's tools lost their luster and relevance but continued to be employed as if nothing had changed. Protests of the war had been overt. Protests in the workplace had been covert, as they continue to be. Unfortunately, this led to the *Leaderless Leadership Syndrome* because:

The structure of work determines the function of work.

The function of work establishes the workplace culture.

The workplace culture seeds the dominant behavior in the workplace.

Management is the architect of this delicate balance. So, it falls to executive vision, leadership, and competence as to whether an organization is purposeful or flounders. Modern workers have a passion for work when it is designed for success. Conversely, they are apathetic when it is not. Purposeful work is not a matter of serendipity nor does it happen in a vacuum. It is a question of executive purpose and leadership. There is far too much evidence this reality is not perceived.

James R. Fisher, Jr., *Six Silent Killers: Management's Greatest Challenge* (1998)

Any organization has 15 percent of hard chargers and 15 percent of foot draggers with the other 70 percent falling in the middle as safe hires doing what told to do but little more.

The corporate toolkit may have worked 50-years ago, but it no longer works today. Incredibly, few will dispute this, but still, there is little movement to change or inclination to buck the trend.

Interventions

During the 1942-1945 wartime period, where less than 10 percent of American workers were college trained, and less than 50 percent high school graduates, where workers were dependent on management for direction, where decision making was indisputably an exclusive managerial right, and where position power trumped knowledge power, workers jumped through hoops even if the hoops bordered on the ridiculous.

Workers were treated like children and expected to act like children, as only managers were the grown-ups. Workers shied away from challenging the authority of the lowest supervisor or going over that supervisor's head to complain. The way to stay out of trouble was to keep your head down.

The boom continued through the 1950s and 1960s, then the calamitous 1970s came. The United States was losing the war in Vietnam; American markets were declining in electronic parts, computers, glassware, televisions, microwaves, and finally, automobiles. Japan, South Korea, and Singapore were making quality products more cheaply and reliably than those made in the US.

Panic set in, as corporations looked desperately for answers. They studied their South East Asia competition only to discover they were using American quality control technology, expertise that fit nicely into Asian group-oriented cultures but ignored by American companies.

A period of schizophrenia followed. First, there was a wild dash to superimpose the Asian success model on Americans without recognizing the clash between the group and individualistic norms. Secondly, blue-collar workers dominated the Asian workforce whereas they did not in the American workplace. By 1980, already, American professionals outnumbered four to one every Asian professional.

The 20 percent of American blue-collar workers responded to this intervention as they did to *Elton Mayo's intervention in 1927 at the Hawthorne Works at the Western Electric Company in Chicago*. The workers were flattered for the attention. Fast-forward to the 1980s and these workers didn't mind the problem solving being confined to cosmetic change (e.g., workstation design, reducing noise, changing lighting). This was not the case with professionals who saw this attention as "by the numbers" rote exercises.

A stream of interventions followed: *Total Quality Management, Quality Control Circles, Quality of Work, Quality of Work Life, Total Employee Involvement*, and *Participative Empowerment Management*. Essentially, nothing changed.

These were programs. Quality is a process, a mindset that depends on the integrity of the supportive structure. This was not developed. So, everything drifted to how it had been freeze-framed in 1945 nostalgia, which compounded worker frustration.

That said, work has changed dramatically from brawn to brainpower, and workers have changed intellectually with this. Now, knowledge workers occupy 90 percent of the critical mass in high-tech industries. Yet, except for these industries, most workplace cultures remain in cadence with the distant past.

Given this scenario, professionals complain about how things are instead of realizing they can change them, still looking to the company for relief of their anxieties as dependent children and still behaving as dissonant workers.

Management is not leadership. It has opted for pyramid climbing by always campaigning for the next position never having time to do the job paid to do. Now that the pyramid is collapsing and with it its position power, it has become avaricious to the extreme. Why, then, should there be any surprise when those that climb to the top can't lead?

Leadership combines vision and values with resolve and power.

Henry Ford and Thomas Edison demonstrated leadership inconspicuously and quietly.

Ford didn't invent the automobile or the assembly line. He used both to create the working middle class that could afford to buy his automobile by using the assembly line to make the vehicles cheaply.

Edison didn't invent the light bulb but created the first practical incandescent light. Whereas others confined their efforts to laboratory applications of light bulbs, he concentrated on its commercial use in homes and businesses by mass-producing long-lasting light bulbs. A system of generating and distributing electricity followed, which led to the establishment of the first electric utility in the world at the Pearl Street Station in New York City.

Ford and Edison were known as something of curmudgeons and hardly charismatic figures. Leadership with them wasn't an act but a behavior.

What is construed as leadership today is a managerial process of refining what is known with little interest in venturing into the unknown. As such, it is obsessed with competition and therefore imitative, unimaginative, predictable, and myopic. Trapped in this habit of mind often leads to corporate fraud and malfeasance with those in leadership roles using their positions unseemly. This is not new. Machiavelli wrote about it 500-years ago.

Who created these sybarites? Society did. Who structured organizations to spawn them? Society did that as well. Who is society? We are. Top executive pay that has skyrocketed from 100 to as much as 1,000 times that of the average worker didn't happen without an assist. Our culture provided that, and right at a time when leadership is rising in Ford-Edison fashion from the bottom of the tree.

This is truly unfortunate as companies were as late as 1975 still weren't tarnished by runaway executive compensation, as ethical standards were high and maintained with few exceptions. Everything seemed to unravel with compensation going crazy to parallel the cyberspace era. Lost in the shuffle has been true leadership, as no one seems in charge with everyone's head down in some electronic distraction.

Professional Workers

Information technology has transformed knowledge workers into a breed apart, as work, workers, and the workplace have been made redundant with no efficacious model to replace this vestigial organ. Central corporate control with its phalanx of electronic tributaries is also redundant as is its management. This dinosaur is a relic fit for the museum.

A possible antidote is guided autonomy of workers in a more natural setting where cooperation and trust and connection materialize by sponsors without hidden agendas.

It is passé for workers to be simply polite, obedient, docile, uncritical, submissive, apologetic, and dependent, with no voice in the decision-making. No longer can we afford for workers to be switched-off and passive on the job and proactive off the job. No longer can we afford for them to behave like children at work and adults at home.

Executives protest, "Why can't workers behave like adults? We give them everything!" Not true.

Professionals are seldom treated as equals when they are often more than equal to those in charge. To add insult to injury, professionals are monitored, tracked, and watched with surveillance cameras, plainly indicating they are not trusted, not respected, and not accepted as colleagues. Professionals are deliberately pitted against each other for pay increases and promotion as well as for perks, driving them into passive-resistive behaviors.

Managers have created a system that predictably brings out the worst in these professionals. While they are the soul of the machine, executives run off with the proceeds, as if that is the most natural thing to do.

It took the first half of the twentieth century for management to flourish and the second half of the century for management, as we know it, to move perilously close to extinction.

Management acumen at mid-century was deemed leadership when it was a survival strategy. Even at its apogee it misread workers as being interested only in a paycheck, motivated only by self-interest. Work has always been workers' true interest, professionals in particular. The work is the reward.

In the Shadow of the Courthouse, Memoir of the 1940s Written as a Novel, 2nd Edition (2013) – Originally published in 2003.

In the Shadow of the Courthouse invites the reader to this 'rites of passage' of passage memoir. Imagine coming of age (8 to 13) in Clinton, Iowa in the middle of the United States in the middle of the 20th century (1942 -1947) in the middle of this farm belt community of 33,000 snuggled against the muddy banks of the Mississippi River during World War Two, and in the Shadow of the Clinton County Courthouse with its magnificent four-faced clock chiming the time every half hour, and looking down on you no matter you might be.

It is in this working-class climate that the author came of age in the shadow of that courthouse while the nation struggled to come of age in the shadow of the atomic bomb.

There was no television; no mega sports. Nor were there big new automobiles on the streets or manicured lawns in the community. There were movies, high school sports, and the Industrial Baseball League where men too young or too old to go to the war played baseball for the fun of it. Clintonians, as everyone was known, had victory gardens, drove their old jalopies, took the bus, or rode their bicycles to work.

It was a time when the four faces of the Clinton County Courthouse clock threw a metaphorical shadow over young people's lives. This made certain that they would have no excuse for being late for meals made essentially out of victory garden staples.

The courthouse neighborhood, which is the focus of this story, had most stay-at-home mothers in two-parent families. Few parents managed to get beyond grammar school, nearly all worked in Clinton factories or on the railroad. Divorce was as foreign as an ancestral language.

It was a time when Clinton families during atrocious summer heating spells could be found sleeping in Riverview Park adjacent to the Mississippi River, watching the river barges passing in the night. It was not uncommon for people to leave their windows open and their doors unlocked, and their bicycles on the side of the house, and if they had automobiles, keys in the car, secure in the knowledge that neither neighbor nor stranger would disturb their possessions.

In winter, schools never closed even when snowbanks were four feet high.

In the Shadow of the Courthouse is a narrative snapshot of core neighborhood activities against the backdrop of the courthouse, St. Patrick's Church and School, Riverview Stadium, downtown Clinton, and uptown Lyons, Bluff Boulevard, Hoot Owl Hollow, Mount St. Clare College, and Convent, Mill Creek, Beaver Slough, Joyce Slough, the churches and schools and hospitals throughout the city, the United States Army Schick Hospital, which brought the war to this place tending battlefield casualties, the USO, the Chicago & North Western Railroad, Clinton Foods, DuPont, and many other industries, working 24/7 to the war effort as seen through the impressionistic eyes of the author as a boy from age eight to thirteen.

It was a time when kids created their play, as parents were too tired or too involved in the struggle to make a living to pay them much mind. Clinton youngsters would never again know such Darwinian freedom or its concomitant brutality again.

This is not a history of the times. Nor is this a novel in the conventional sense, but rather the recollections of a time, place, and circumstance through the author's confessed imperfect vision. In the Shadow of the Courthouse promises to awaken the child in the reader whatever his age or time.

In the Shadow of the Courthouse
Memoir of The 1940s Written As A Novel

James R. Fisher, Jr.
Author of The Taboo Against Being Your Own Best Friend

From the pages of IN THE SHADOW OF THE COURTHOUSE

I'm told that many authors ponder the first line of their novels sometimes for months feeling that it is that critical to their story. I must confess that was not the case with me. When I learned of the death of my boyhood friend and courthouse neighbor, Bobby Witt, which occurred on August 27, 1990, it jarred me so hard that I immediately wrote down this line:

The first day of my life was when I was eight-years-old and I met Bobby Witt.

My family had just moved into the courthouse neighborhood from Lyons, which is *North Clinton* (Iowa).

It would be thirteen years before this book would be published, taking more than a score of visits to Clinton from my home in Tampa, Florida, some thousands of miles away, to interview contemporaries of the period 1942 to 1947, or essentially the war years of the *Second World War.*

Moreover, some 100 *Clintonians* growing up during this period were happy to tell their story as best remembered. This also found me a regular visitor to *The Clinton County Library* to review the microfiche of *The Clinton Herald* of these years, as well as making many visits to *The Clinton County Historical Society* to peruse its extensive archives. I also made a point to visit *Mount St. Clare College & Convent*, which was the residence of the *Sisters of St. Francis* who taught at St. *Patrick's Catholic School* during the years when Bobby Witt and I attended from the fourth through the eighth grade. A surprising number of these nuns were still alive and living in a splendid retirement home where I would visit them when in Clinton.

The Clinton County Courthouse, for a boy not yet a teenager during World War Two, is not only majestic but mythical. It found me on one of my visits, sitting in my car on Sixth Avenue North in front of this courthouse writing this poem:

If I were a poet . . .

I would confess I have never lost my affection for this edifice. It was like a parent that never wavered, never changed. I am sitting here now, reflecting on the fact that it is more than forty years since I spent any time with this dear old friend.

If I were a poet, I would give this edifice metaphorical significance, like a giant knight, standing ever at attention to protect my neighborhood from itself and the dangers outside.

If I were a poet, I would see it as a Greek god, an Adonis, a Zeus, a mighty warrior who never falters from its vigilance.

If I were a poet, I would sing the praises of this frozen music, this enchanting melody which never varies in my head; this quiet dignity; this sculptured perfection; this sensible grace as common as a pair of old shoes.

If I were a poet, I would wonder why we could have such stability, such reasoned continence against the harsh reality of a tumultuous world, as it has not varied for me one iota from what it was a half-century ago.

If I were a poet, I would declare that the tower, the time, and the psychology of its movement are frozen like magic so that wherever I go, it is "stop time" to my mind.

If I were a poet, I would tell the world that it has been so important in making this fumbling, stumbling, this bumbling individual called "me," always feel a mystical anchor in my roots of being.

If I were a poet, I would exalt its unique character with Vivaldi's "Four Seasons" to dramatize how the earth around may change, but the spirit within remains forever constant.

If I were a poet, I would note that men live and die, but that this structure is immortal because it exists beyond nature.

If I were a poet, I would sit here and wonder as I am now, over the happiness I feel for having the opportunity to once again ponder the regard I hold for it, and finally,

If I were a poet, I would want the world to know of the many lives that this edifice, this sentinel has influenced in the course of my fleeting life. How many young who are now old have been given succor and sustenance, and the semblance of order in their lives because they have once lived IN THE SHADOW OF THE COURTHOUSE?

One Clintonian interviewed, Ron McGauvran, a high school classmate at Clinton High, and a Clinton businessman, put this book in perspective:

For Clintonians, "In the Shadow of the Courthouse" will remind them of many things long forgotten. For others, it will give them a sense of what it was like growing up when their parents and grandparents were young. For everyone, it will reacquaint them with their youth and how they dealt with growing up, the naiveté and fumbling for an understanding of life.

Confident Thinking: A Silver Bullet for an Unconscious Age, 1st Edition (2014)

Confidence comes from thinking and problem solving that works. This leads to a sense of moving in the right direction.

The prescription proposed here is no radical theory of logic and semantics, but simply provides keys to awake in the reader his reality and to take charge.

We have witnessed the limitations of "value-free analysis" and of rational thinking in the tradition of Socrates. That said we have gone through a period of unconscious incompetence spawning a Culture of Comfort where bosses purport to have the answers requiring workers to be passive and reactive to their dictums. When that reached the point of organizational disaster, whether then reexamining the inequality of the distribution of power and control between managers and workers, corrective interventions led instead to conscious incompetence as the Culture of Complacency.

Work has changed with workers with it going from brawn to brainpower, from manual to mental, from set norms to constantly changing requirements, with workers now predominantly professionally trained. Still, the matter of managing, motivating, mobilizing, and manipulating workers has not changed. Moreover, not only has the color of workers color changed but the gender and ethnicity of workers as well. Now, women and people of color are increasingly a compelling presence.

Critical thinking, or thinking in terms of what is already known has proven inadequate if not redundant whereas creative thinking, or thinking in terms of what is not known or is not immediately apparent but can be found out is becoming increasingly relevant in a world of constant change.

The shift can be described as workers going from knowers to learners, tellers to listeners, no longer searching for answers but in creating solutions. Emphasis is shifting from process to perception, objectivity to subjectivity, from facts to feelings, from other-directedness to self-direction, from celebrating information to exploring the value of ideas, from linear to nonlinear thinking, from breaking problems down to seeing them holistically, from multiculturalism to uni-culturalism, from arrogance to humility in the problem-solving.

Confident Thinking is looking forward rather than back embracing change rather than being obsessed with stability by promoting conscious rather than unconscious engagement.

First Edition

From the pages of CONFIDENT THINKING

BELIEVE IN YOURSELF COMPLETELY
HAVE FAITH IN YOUR ABILITY TO DO
THEN DESIRE WHAT YOU DO!

A wise man will desire no more than he may get justly, use soberly, distribute cheerfully, and leave contentedly. The passions and desires, like the two twists of a rope, mutually mix one with the other, and twine inextricably round the heart; producing good, if moderately indulged; but certain destruction if suffered to become inordinate.

Richard E. Burton, Nineteenth-Century American Author

THE REGIMENTATION

FROM OUR EARLIEST memory we are doing what others tell us to do and what these significant others tell us is important, not only to do but what to think. Consequently, there is little time to know the rhythm of our hearts.

Added to this is the constant bombardment of television, which subliminally and aggressively engages our attention, creating a desire for what is packaged in a way to make "whatever" most wanted. If this were not enough, we are now exposed to the Internet, and handheld electronic devices with digital games that have nonsense caricatures of aggression, intended to energize our animal instincts, to crush, plunder, destroy, and punish those characters the electronic designers have declared the enemy. All this is innocent fun until it becomes translated into community violence, insensitive to life, limb, and property.

If this were not enough, the noise has been declared music; noise that its creators insist is art. This destroys our eardrums and bombards our senses with bad language and even worse images, offensive to our nature as loving and caring human beings. We are told by its promoters that this is not harmful to us without explaining how it is good for us.

With this constant discordant noise, we grow old, but never find time to grow up, seeking refuge from this synthetic distraction in games, drugs, and other recreational excesses, remaining unreceptive to the music of

Mother Nature; to the singing of birds, chirping of insects, the patter of rain, or the sight of dancing clouds across the sky.

We are programmed to become strangers to ourselves almost from the moment of birth, responding to the agenda of others, who claim they have our best interests at heart when all too often it is only their own. They place us in a cage of their good intentions and then wonder why we smile through clenched teeth or fail to develop the gumption to protest. There are many clues as to why.

We are thirsty sponges for all this attention; for all this instruction; for all this noise and pontification. We think our motivation is love when it is only counter-dependence. It differs little from the wild birds who are fed by tourists, eventually losing their instinct to forage for food on their own. We absorb it all, without complaint or comprehension, docile and agreeable unable to do otherwise.

We are amorphous tissue and bone molded into a form susceptible to the popular norms of our time supplied in nurturing care by those we love, respect, fear and admire as if we have no will of our own. Consequently, much of our early training has a tinge of anxiety to it, not because of what and who we are, which is not clear to us, but because significant others unwittingly cause us to be anxious and unsure.

They have their reputation, which is already established, and we are meant in our innocence to protect that reputation by proxy as willing indiscriminate sponges, giving attention to their biases and then treating them as if our own. So, the first breakdown in belief in self is suffered before we know what that means.

Much is made when we first walk, talk, or show mental or physical dexterity. Likewise, the concern is shown when we seem self-centered with little evidence of altruistic inclination. We are expected to be or approximate mirror images of our DNA elders.

Self-interest and aggression are discouraged when self-interest and aggression are the foundation of *confident thinking* in terms of belief in oneself.

Well-meaning though these significant others may be, they introduce us to a cultural disease: "compare and compete." It has crippled our civilization producing dull, imitative, insensitive, mediocre, burned-out and stereotypical individuals who are devoid of initiative, imagination, originality, and spontaneity.

Great art, philosophy, music, literature, and science have been created by the exception, not the rule. Albert Einstein turned physics on its head after it had been coasting for 300 years. Technology has replaced all that once was deemed art, music, philosophy, literature, and science with its game plan.

So, almost from the beginning of our consciousness, we are aware of how well someone else does something and how poorly we do the same. Our attention is not only other-directed but our self-approval as well. We must search for what is important instead of allowing it to surface naturally in us, something that is buried deep in our soul, crying out to be heard.

We are instructed to be friendly, not shown how to be our own best friend. We are told how important love is but exposed to the constant drum roll of sex and eroticism, which has little to do with love. We are told to seek freedom from fear but never to embrace it, which is the only way such freedom can be realize. We are told to seek perfection, but creativity is derived from our imperfection. We are reminded that to be alone is the nature of loneliness, which only leads to depression when one is never alone if comfortable in one's own company. We are told greed is a need when it is insatiable want. Greed can never be satisfied, but need can. We are conditioned to fear death when it is our life that we fear. How could we fear death when it is unknown? We are conditioned to be polite, never to be candid, which insinuates it is better to lie, thereby alienating us from our self.

THE BREAKING FREE

We are constantly reminded that we ought to become this or that, and not to be satisfied with just being ourselves. We're counseled that progress is our most important product. This never gives us time to be content, and being content is the only place happiness can be found. Yet "happiness" has become a pejorative that we should avoid like the plague, even while it is celebrated. We must constantly be "becoming," which means never arriving.

Becoming lives alongside the illusion of progress. Becoming thrives on ambition; yearns to be loved; depends on the approval of others; feels emotionally drained; craves rewards; performs for pay; and dances to the company tune, while living on borrowed time with borrowed money.

On the other hand, "being" lives comfortably in our skin. Reality is its home, where it owes nothing to others; nothing to sacrifice to earn their approval; no need to demonstrate our worthiness to demand attention; nowhere to go but where we are; no concern about "Big Brother's" watchful eye as no one's head in any direction is more or less sacred than our own.

That said our friends and relatives, peers and acquaintances compete and compare with us, as do our parents, teachers, and siblings. Competing starts at an early age. It first happens in the home, then in the school, then on to the playground, as we quickly establish the relativity of skills among our playmates. Unfortunately, such assessments are based on narrow parameters of our potential. If magnified early on, we may never grow into ourselves because we're always trying to be and please others. What others decide we are may not be best for us or even true. We may end up reproving ourselves for the neglect of our potential when we have never addressed its possibilities.

If we are slow of foot or hand, don't see well, or don't have good hand-eye coordination, peers will be quick to remind us of such shortcomings, and painfully so, choosing us last when in games, or not choosing us at all. Strangely, this may become our salvation, as we have little choice but to become acquainted with ourselves.

The pitfall, however, is that we may drift towards others equally spurned but without insight into their gifts. This is not a time to brood or think of ourselves as losers or be obsessed with the winners who rejected us. This is a time to introduce us to ourselves as persons.

A bigger game is taking place within us. It has a rhythm and range, a character and composition unique to us that differs from those from whom we have drifted apart. The mark of our individuality is stamped on us, and we now have the opportunity to find out what it is telling us.

When we become preoccupied with others, the "who" and "what" that they are, compared to the "who" and "what" that we are can be consumed in adolescent jealousy. Realistically, some allowance must be made for this angst as few of us are likely to escape it when we are young.

Jealousies with maturity can eventually go away, but envy never dies. To envy someone is to willingly poison the heart with something we can never have and never be because we are not the other person, inflicting a lasting scar on our psyche while nourishing an embittering lifetime mindset.

With those so inclined, there is a tendency from the youngest age to exaggerate the coveted qualities of others, whatever they may be, without appreciation the qualities that one possesses that are equally significant.

One thing is certain: people of great achievements also possess great weaknesses. No one escapes personal weakness. People make headlines when their greatness becomes public knowledge. We expect these people to be less vulnerable, which is to say, less human than we are, when they tend to be more human, meaning more flawed. Their ambition finds them taking great risks to scale to heady heights while fighting constant wars with their demons in battles that sublimate into greatness. It is because, not despite their demons, that they are great.

Some buy into the idea of their celebrity, seeing themselves as untouchables, basking in the idolatry, taking their genius to be self-evident when it is a gift from God who has a sense of humor. He inserts in their bonnet unsavory temptations that play on their self-ignorance that often leads to their ultimate undoing.

People of tremendous ability must also battle tremendous demons. If these demons are not monitored, they inevitably lead to disaster and despair.

Greatness is the play of the angels and demons of our nature clashing within us with creative verve. Without this thunder, nothing of consequence would find the light of day. So, we should be charitable to the most gifted among us because the war these people fight every day is a war that would humble most of us very quickly.

People we deem "great," who manage to somehow earn such recognition, are the same people who learn at an early age to hide what they are not. They bury their misgivings, their fears of being inadequate, frauds or pretenders, yet, at the same time, excelling despite themselves. They are always as surprised as we are at their success.

Fame makes them easy targets for sycophants who magnify their strengths and minimize their weaknesses to their hedonistic advantage. That is why celebrities are often found to have clay feet, having bought into their celebrity as a manifestation of themselves when it is only a façade. They accomplish this by developing the unique skill of placing the focus on their strengths away from their weaknesses. They offset the emotional deficit of weakness by appearing different than the rest of us to justify the adoration, envy, love, and hate that they engender when they are more like us than different from us.

They step out of the ordinary to appear extraordinary, succeeding in promoting idolatry, envy, and jealousy. We compare ourselves to them and compete with an image that is not only unreal but surreal. We are seduced by an image of a person we don't know and most likely will never meet, at the expense of discovering our precious uniqueness.

In a celebrity culture, nothing is what it seems as others define everything that should matter making us strangers to ourselves as persons for the adoring attention. Celebrity worship is a sickness that becomes a cultural norm when the majority makes it so.

DESIRE IN THE DOUBLE BIND JUNGLE OF WANT

Confident Thinking recognizes that we must cut through this baffling obsession to discover what we desire. Desire is the noblest aspect of *Confident Thinking*. It becomes however problematic when we want what we don't need, and need what we don't want. Once the desire is driven by want, there is never enough. Want, as with greed, can never be satisfied. Want always needs more.

Want is a hole in the psyche, a prison of self-en-cage-ment. Want is the road to self-destruction. Want can ultimately destroy everything near and dear to us. Want is the constant mantra of the advertiser, the pundit, the television guru, and the criminal. Want is the separation of the soul from the body falling into the bottomless pit between yesterday and tomorrow with no bridge to today.

Want is the double bind and wishful behavior of the immature individual running on the mania of unquenchable demand.

This occurs when we look for others to fight our battles and carry us to safety through the hostile wilderness of life. When we attempt to do for others what they best do for themselves, we weaken their resolve and make them emotionally cripples. This is so because we devalue them as persons. The same holds for us if we allow someone else to carry our burden. Only we can carry that burden for we created it by the choices we have made.

The double bind of wanting destroys. It fills our hospitals and rehabilitation centers with lifestyle complaints and enslaves the mind with delusions of grandeur.

- The enslaved mind is *passive-receptive.* It sees itself becoming a "big shot," whereas a free mind is *active-productive* and creative.

- The enslaved mind takes; the free mind gives.

- The enslaved mind pleads to get its way; the free mind takes the initiative.

- The enslaved mind seeks security by conforming; the free mind is non-attached and embraces freedom.

- The enslaved mind is obsessed with the *superiority-inferiority* mindset; the free mind has no desire to impress and puts no one on a pedestal.

- The enslaved mind has placed its *center-of-gravity* in others; the free mind's *center-of-gravity* is within.

- The enslaved mind follows rules to the nth degree no matter how ridiculous; the free mind uses its discretionary power to validate or challenge the rules.

- The enslaved mind imitates; the free mind improvises.

- The enslaved mind is impressed with appearances; the free mind cuts through the façade.

The double bind of the enslaved mind is like a coyote chasing two rabbits at once, going in opposite directions, whereas the free mind is like water that can flow into and around everything regardless of shape or size. It fits into anything.

The free mind can best be illustrated by the fact that it manipulates circumstances as called for, as well as things, but not people. The free mind refuses to trap itself in old forms, traditions, customs, and programming. It understands that its programming is the culprit that enslaves.

Want, then, is the ultimate punishment of self-haters. They strive "to please others," which they never do with little inclination to understand much less please themselves. Want is a cagey game of self-deception, thinking they are pleasing themselves when they attempt to emulate someone they admire at the expense of being themselves. They are perfect fodder for the advertiser, the con, the flatterer, the sycophant, and the bully.

The need is fundamental to their existence and is fed by natural desire. We need food, shelter, clothing, human contact, love, and work, but want separates us into groups, classes, categories, and classifications. Advertisers know this; housing developers know this; social architects of culture know this; and so we imitate those we envy most by conforming to their tastes, only on a reduced economic scale often at the expense of our heritage, customs, culture, and nature.

Evidence of this: every American large city looks the same; every village the same; every new community the same; every place looks like every other place; everyone dresses like everyone else; everyone eats what everyone else eats; everyone works where everyone else works doing what everyone else is doing; and everyone mates and marries or relates to others like everyone else does.

Even the least expensive car looks like the most expensive car; the least expensive clothes look like the most expensive clothes. When the need becomes synonymous with want, there is no longer originality; no longer authenticity; no longer real contrast between what is real and what is not. It is an artificial existence spinning out of control, and no one seems to notice because the focus is always on the spinning and not on the spinner.

There is no possibility of *Confident Thinking* when what we are doing is not what we desire to be doing. It lacks legitimacy when it is someone else's idea; something we bought into a long time ago and have come to think it was our idea. The evidence of the falsity of this want is revealed in a new promotion as little satisfaction is derived as want presses on for the next promotion.

Don't confuse organizational pyramid climbers with doers. Climbing is a full-time and all-out proposition in which there is no time to do, only time to take credit for what others do. Climbers are obsessed with getting to the top. They are hungry and full of want. They were born wanting; they live for want fulfillment, and they will die wanting still more. If you were to ask them, what their purpose in life is, they would say, "to get to the top." But that is not a purpose. That is a want. They do not know nor want to know why they climb. They just do.

Doers do not seek anything. They are builders. They create and shape their world inside themselves, which has little resemblance to the world outside. They could be billionaires but it was never their desire to be billionaires. They desired to create something good for the world. They explore, discover, produce, and build-out of the fullness and independence of that desire. They live in a state of excitement as they look to the horizon to discover the unfolding of the unknown. They believe in themselves and that is their secret as that finds them able to believe in others.

More Recently Published Books

When you are inclined to write, and feel you have ideas to share, ideas that may be out-of-step with those who would turn human conscience, consciousness, reflection, thought, and feeling into a new instrument of Artificial Intelligence (AI), you write because you believe in God, believe in humanity, and have a sense that feeling is as important or more important than facts. Then, there is the added reason: because you can.

What follows is a representative of these additional writings along with their publishing date, along with their covers, and a brief explanation of why they have been published, not in any suspected order.

ERIC HOFFER & THE
FISHER PARADIGM©™

JAMES R.
FISHER Jr.

MIRROR OF THE PSYCHE

Mirror of the Psyche: Eric Hoffer & The Fisher Paradigm (2021). *This is an imagined conversation with Eric Hoffer* (1898 – 1983) with the author's observations in The Fisher Paradigm©™ vis-à-vis similar views of the author Eric Hoffer.

Both authors see the *"terrible 60s"* as being a *watershed moment* where the children of "baby boomers" demonstrated their callous resentment and consuming disrespect of parental authority while rejecting institutional thinking.

These juveniles running amok were nerd cowboys. But if you thought sixty years later that they had disappeared from our psyche, think again.

Now they are running Facebook, Google, Amazon, Microsoft, and Apple with draconian if not absolute control and authority that makes the exploits of the Carnegies, Mellons, Rockefellers, and Fords seem like child's play. Indeed, the "terrible 60s" have never left us. Silicon Valley graduates from the 60s counterculture are now personified in Zuckerberg, Brin, Page, Bezos, Gates, and Job. While rejecting the conventional theology of God, they have created a theology of technology with the engineer their search engine. Now, there is no place for "free will" and no need for individualism. *Mirror of the Psyche* revisits Hoffer to dramatize the dawn of this new era.

The Fisher Paradigm©™ traces the survival of man as Homo sapiens on this earth by featuring the reptilian brain and the power of instinct and intuitive wisdom to gain insight into difficult or even threatening situations. The author demonstrates this thesis by offering meaningful episodes in his professional career as an industrial psychologist and organizational development (OD) consultant.

The author argues in *"Who Put You in the Cage"* (2018) that we put ourselves in our cages. Sadly, once confined, we may reside in these self-conceived cages our entire lives. Without psychiatric or psychotherapy counseling and care, chances are we will blame our situation on everyone but ourselves: our parents, friends, siblings, teachers, priests, bosses or coworkers, everyone but ourselves.

This self-imprisoning can manifest itself as being hateful of others, constantly angry while being jealous or envious of what others are and have. This springs from seeing the world outside our confinement more meaningful and attractive than ours.

We can't manage our money which leads to the cage of debt; we destroy our health by eating, drinking, and smoking too much; we don't know how to say "no" to anyone: our partner, children, parents, and friends when to say "yes" jeopardizes our well-being. Social psychologists penetrate these cages and provide strategies to extricate ourselves from such confinement by presenting a potpourri of case studies.

In *"Ten Creative Stages to Confident Thinking"* (2018), author Fisher asks, "Imagine you have filled all the boxes and filled in all the blanks required according to your chosen career, only to find after experiencing some success you have written into a wall. It could be the technology changing, your mentor leaving the company, souring personal relations, a downturn in the economy, or alas, discovering this is not what you want to do the rest of your working life.

It leaves you as if standing on a rock surveying the future in a fog, saying to yourself, "Is this all there is to life?"

Most of us have been there; most of us have experienced disruption but we have not all seen this as an opportunity to restart our engine to a more satisfying future.

TEN CREATIVE STAGES OF CREATIVE THINKING consider common benchmarks highly successful people have used to leap over this wall from success to continuing success.

In *"The Wisdom of Being Your Own Psychotherapist"* (2019), author Fisher is not demeaning the legitimate role of people who find themselves in some kind of a cage, most likely of their own making. This book addresses what psychologist Bernie Zilbergeld "the shrinking of America" where psychotherapy is a crutch to avoid doing anything constructive about what is troubling you. It is a kind of dependence, prominent with those who refuse to grow up consistent with psychological myths of change, which are discussed in this book.

Confidence in Subtext (2020) argues that the conscious mind is simply a Rolodex primarily processing the content and context of the everyday stimuli we experience, conveniently compatible with what is already in our minds. In conversation, we say the same things about the same things, and without realizing it, are telling the same stories to our friends and partners as if new information. No one is guiltier of this than this author. Yet, it is the subtext of our consciousness where the genie of our soul continues to bombard our consciousness with what is important and what is not. The fact that we don't listen is often at our peril.

As Freud has pointed out it is the subconscious or unconscious where repressed thoughts and denied emotions reside that often play havoc with our conscious lives. Acknowledging and listening to this "voice within" can be liberating as it puts us in touch with our primitive instincts and intuitive understanding of our situation that goes beyond rational intelligence in problem-solving.

This biographical novel was written over fifty years with half of its content published in *"Devlin, A Psychological Novel"* in 2018. It depicts the experiences of an ordinary Midwestern American family that finds itself in 1968 in South Africa during the era of apartheid.

The year 1968 was not only traumatic for the Devlins but the world as it ended the honeymoon of post-World War Two for victorious America. For the United States as well as this family the past was cut from the future with everything being made up whimsically for this family as well as the United States which found itself an imperial power beyond the pale of its comprehension.

Ordinary souls often found themselves enjoying opportunities they never entertained as they were members of The Great Depression, a generation demographically the smallest in the nation's history, which of course meant for a cornucopia of opportunity never before nor never again that would be so abundant.

This segment from the book attempts to illustrate this phenomenon.

The Rosebank Hotel, Johannesburg, Sunday, March 17, 1968

Devlin nursed his coffee as he read *The Rand Daily Mail*. South African author Alan Paton had a piece on the op-ed page. He wondered if it were a rant or true. Paton, an Afrikaner, wrote of the government's handling of the Bantu in libelous terms seeming as much a foreigner in his own country as he was. Jonathan Swift's Ireland came to mind, *"Remove me from this land of slaves where all are fools, and all are knaves, where every knave and fool is bought, yet kindly sells himself for naught."* It was not necessary to be black to feel powerless. No surprise, there wasn't any mention in *The Rand Daily Mail* that today was St. Patrick's Day.

"Dirk, what are you reading?" Devlin looked up to see his wife, Sarah, busy outfitting the children in their Sunday best.

"The Rand Daily Mail, a column on apartheid."

The family was waiting for Dirk's boss, Herbert Benjamin "HB" Myers to pick them up to take them to a "mine dance," whatever that was. It was two weeks since they had arrived in South Africa. Everything was new, strange, and kind of wonderful, but Devlin had a gnawing suspicion he couldn't shake, an uneasiness that he had felt since arriving in the country.

It started when they confiscated his copy of Allen Drury's *A Very Strange Society* at the *Jan Smuts International Airport*, of course, promising to return it, which they had not yet done. It continued with his reading. He had been reading a series of articles on *apartheid* written by Benjamin Pogrund in the *Mail*. Pogrund didn't pull any punches. It was reassuring knowing South Africa enjoyed a free press, but Devlin still couldn't get his mind around the idea of *apartheid*. It nagged at his conscience the way a headache did at his temples throwing off his day.

"Apartheid? Not that again!"

He ignored her sarcasm. "This columnist claims the government is spreading disinformation about its policies toward the Bantu. Most whites, he charges, are left in the dark of what is going on." Certainly, he was. No one in Chicago had prepped him on *apartheid* at orientation for this assignment.

"We've been here for what, fourteen days, and you've already gone heavy on me. Dirk, will you never learn? It's not your problem, not your country!"

"Why are you dressing the kids up? We went to mass last night. HB said to dress casual, remember?"

"Like you listen to him? What a hypocrite!"

True, Devlin was dressed in his uniform of the day; a dark blue pinstripe three-piece business suit, button-down blue shirt with monogram cuff links, pastel-colored tie, and a tie clasp with his Phi Beta Kappa key, and tasseled loafers, his only concession to casualness.

The garb was his security blanket. It put starch in his spine. When you look as young as I do, he thought, younger than you are at least by five years, you have to improvise. Dress the part to play the part! Where would an Irishman be without his uniform?

Sarah looked out the window from their 3rd-floor suite. "We'll need raincoats and umbrellas, but of course we don't have them!"

She, too, suffered from unease but of a different kind. She was already homesick. Here she was the daughter of a journeyman electrician ensconced in a suite of five rooms, two baths, a formal sitting room, and an enclosed balcony with a floor-to-ceiling picture window overlooking the winding driveway in front of the hotel. She was a few thousand miles from Crescent City, Iowa, and the drab two-room apartment of her parents, and her growing up years, and she missed it all. She missed the simple life. It tore at her heart to look at her big lug of a husband, so confident, composed and so at home wherever he found himself. She wished she could hate him, but she couldn't. She couldn't love him either. There wasn't any room anywhere for her feelings.

Devlin joined her at the window. What he saw was the classical elegance of the setting. The Rosebank Hotel was in the center of an upscale suburb of Johannesburg on the corner of Tyrwhitt and Sturdee Avenues. He'd have to check out the origin of those names. Prominent Afrikaner pioneers no doubt. He wondered if some city would one day carry his name on a street. The thought gave him a warm glow. He had to pinch himself sometimes to realize how far he had come in a short thirty years of life, far from the spineless world of his Irish clan, and on his own! Who would have thought -- certainly not his da but most certainly his mother!

"Trust me, Sarah, it'll be a beautiful day! It's still early. South Africa is moving from fall into winter, something that I understand is quite mild."

"What?"

"Everything is upside down in the southern hemisphere. Water goes down the drain counterclockwise, if you've noticed. Winter here on the Transvaal doesn't compare to that of Iowa. We will experience the four seasons, more or less, but nothing like Iowa. Weather is warm year-round but not as warm as Florida, at least that is what the literature says."

"Wonderful," she said, thinking she'd take a harsh Iowa winter any day for this. "That's another thing you failed to tell us." How could she tell him she didn't care; why did he always have to be on, so grand about things that only irritated her?

Sensing her unease, he added, "I found it by reading." He wanted to say, you could find it out the same way but didn't. He even wanted to say, you could have stayed at home in Louisville with the kids, but didn't, knowing that would positively have ruined the day, but he had to admit the thought had some appeal.

The day was indeed cold sending a shiver through him as he spoke. There was the sweet smell of rain in the air that he loved as he looked down from the window opened a crack as his boss drove into view.

He looked at his Rolex, a tick past 6 a.m., and had to admit the day did look gray with the morning dew reflecting chiaroscuro shadows off the streetlights. Devlin wasn't much into nature but liked the contrived ambiance of the landscaped lawn, statuesque trees, and carefully trimmed shrubs along the boulevard below. Tidiness was managed control.

"Give it a rest, will you? You're always reading." She stifled the anger in her voice for she wanted the day to go well. She didn't want to be a shrew but wondered how she could act happy when she was not? *He's so full of himself he hasn't a clue that I hate this place. Everything is always all about him, what about me? Don't I count for something? Stop it! Look on the good side. Despite it being cold and wet, we're doing something as a family for a change.* Yes! Her heart raced as she saw Mr. Meyers in his leased Cadillac circle into the driveway below. "He's here!"

*　　*　　*

HB let the attendant park his car, saying something, then walked slump-shouldered into the building. Devlin watched him. He was a small man, small in stature with small hands and feet, a receding hairline of thin black hair already turning gray although not yet fifty, but a man with a huge brain. He was Devlin's mentor, friend, and boss.

Both men were accidents of post-World War II America, two cerebral types pushed into unfamiliar roles of men-of-action simply by chance. American industry was exploding and no place more than in the chemical industry, which the United States owned internationally.

They were bench chemists by profession. HB had been a Polychem R&D chemist when it was a $20 million company. He was a graduate of *Wabash College* in Crawfordsville, Indiana with a master's degree from *Purdue University* in Lafayette, Indiana. Devlin had been an R&D chemist with Midland Chemical, a Fortune 100 company, an operation located in his hometown. He was a graduate of the *State University of Iowa* in Iowa City in chemical engineering with a master's degree from the same institution in chemistry.

HB's progress was stepwise from research to technical service to corporate sales on the strength of his technical prowess alone. He ran Polychem's *Industrial Sales Division*, never having been in sales, and then *Polychem's International Division*, when he had never traveled west of the Mississippi River or east of Pittsburgh, until now. Polychem was xenophobic promoting only from within.

Devlin's route to the executive ranks was equally haphazard to the point of being implausible He joined Polychem less than six years before, and then only as a stopgap measure in route to a Ph.D. With a wife and two small children to support, he needed to earn quick money, choosing technical sales, before assuming a fellowship in theoretical chemistry at *Wesleyan University* in Middletown, Connecticut.

The idea of sales came when Midland Chemical's director of research asked him to give a Saturday tour of the plant's multi-facilities to

Madison Avenue advertising executives. Before working in R&D, Devlin had spent five summers while at university working in all the company's chemical processing operations.

"You have a knack for explaining chemistry in laymen's terms," the director said. "We certainly don't want to intimidate them."

At the end of the tour, one of the executives asked him what he did. He told him. "You don't belong in research," he said, "you belong in sales." It was on the strength of that comment that he joined Polychem to temporarily exploit that assumed talent.

Devlin dreamed of becoming the next James Watson in theoretical chemistry model building his way to fame and fortune. Watson had done it with the double helix of DNA. Besides, he saw himself as a washout as a bench chemist, able to manipulate complex variables but incapable of creating the instrumentation necessary for experiments. He sensed he would be a great chemist beyond the lab. It was not to happen.

HB found a niche as Polychem's everyman, which meant never being able to say "no" to any request. This amplified his curse in decision-making – he never had enough data! On the other hand, he was a born mediator projecting a charming manner and a cooperative spirit that put others at ease. He was wise being able to see all sides of an argument but seldom able to resolve an issue. He could calm warring factions but was ill-placed when it came to making critical decisions and he knew it. He needed someone to front for him and take the heat and risk to compensate for his analytical detachment.

It was the nature of the Devlin connection that they were alike but different. HB was a talented bench chemist. Devlin was an ambitious dreamer. HB was a 'true blue' company man who valued himself as his superiors valued him, a composite of everything they thought or said about him. It never occurred to him to question the company's will or the prudence of its actions, much less the ethics of its pursuits. Devlin questioned everything and the motives of everybody.

As fate often plays tricks on us, HB found his brains came in handy as a company strategist, but he had no stomach for playing badass games when the situation demanded. Devlin had a flair for reading people, taking risks, and playing the heavy with no second thoughts. He wouldn't hesitate to get in the face of anyone, senior management included, when he felt compromised.

No surprise, he was reluctantly promoted into management in the *Industrial Division* on the strength of his sales, as he was generally disliked and feared by those around him, but not by HB. Devlin was seen as his salvation. He plucked him out of the field and promoted him to vice president, leapfrogging over four intermediate executive positions, reporting directly to him.

This was an unprecedented company move, but an indicator of HB's clout and his recognized need. Devlin was the iron fist to his velvet glove, and despite what others thought, the match enjoyed unprecedented success across Europe and South America with South Africa the latest challenge.

On the strength of his legendary if unconventional sales, Devlin continued to excel in acquiring major accounts and as a developer of people. His enemies saw him as a maverick and a ticking "time bomb," but not HB.

Devlin was loyal to himself and then to his family and church in that order. He knew he had strong opinions, which were a double-edged sword. It provided perspective and detachment but at the expense of being inclined to be abrasive.

He was suspicious of everyone in the world beyond himself. West coast people were hedonists and dreamers; East coast people thought they were smarter than everyone and behaved as if the United States never grew beyond the thirteen colonies. The South was still fighting the *Civil War* finding new ways to keep Negroes in their place. Only people from the Midwest were real. Nobody there was any better than anyone else. He was a card-carrying Midwesterner, as was HB.

Devlin had little regard for praise but did have a desire for calm, which for him was like chasing a phantom. His drive was to harness his natural talent. Failing that he felt his life was meaningless.

He hated any kind of waste, detesting anyone who flaunted his talent. He was not into revenge when deceived, but would never forget or forgive a transgression. His punishment was narcissistic: he would have nothing to do with that person again.

The subtle difference between HB and Devlin was a gulf that left the two men bound together by fate but separated from understanding. The WASP shadow of expectation hounded HB, while the Catholic shroud of waste harassed Devlin.

Devlin could never be confused with a hardy fellow well-meant. He had a reputation for shooting from the hip, a brooder but dedicated problem solver. His actions weren't always predictable. He believed it easier to ask forgiveness than permission. Nor did logic limit his problem-solving as he had confidence in his intuition. He liked to say he was a thinking feeler rather than a cognitive thinker. This alarmed others, and confused HB. They couldn't argue with his results. Many preferred to see him simply "as lucky."

Devlin was happiest when engaged in problem-solving and thought nothing of the hours involved. In one sense, he was level-headed, and in another, not. This meant he rarely changed his mind while knowing ideas could be traps of which he was the author.

During World War II, the American military needed specialty water treatment chemicals for railroad locomotives, military tanks, ships, and airplanes across the globe. Polychem had the technology, know-how, and products to satisfy these requirements. *The US Department of Defense* (DOD) provided fledgling Polychem with access to these far-flung markets. Once WWII was over, these outposts became manufacturing and distribution centers in such places as Venezuela,

Canada, Mexico, Great Britain, France, Germany, Italy, and South Africa.

A quarter-century after the war (1968), *Polychem International, Inc.* was on the brink of $100 million in sales but suffering a critical shortage of high talent. HB and Devlin rose from otherwise modest careers to fill that void.

So, Get Started! Write Your Own Book!

Like many things you've thought of doing, but you were waiting for the "right time" to get started, writing is like that. Often the "right time" never surfaces as so many other things demand your attention.

Writing is a singular pursuit and requires being comfortable with yourself in the company of the swirling words cascading through your consciousness, waiting to appear in black and white as thoughts now visible that belongs only to you.

There never was a time when creating your work can find itself in print or in an e-book, such as that provided by Amazon.com's Kindle Self-Publishing Authors Library.

Remember, every budding author, amateur or otherwise, has been where you are "right now!"

So, get started and write your own book.

ABOUT THE AUTHOR

Many readers have had to first make a living before being able in good conscience to write. Similarly, author James R. Fisher, Jr. followed an eclectic career working career as an empiricist even before he acquired academic credentials in the discipline of social and industrial psychology. He writes mainly in this genre relative to working professionals noting the role reversal between management/managers and workers/professionals as *knowledge power* now supersedes *position power* in the workplace.

Besides writing in this genre, he is a novelist having published a memoir as a novel (*In the Shadow of the Courthouse*) and a novel of South Africa during Apartheid (*Devlin: A Psychological Novel*).

Fisher commenced his career in the industrial organization as a summer laborer at *Standard Brands, Inc.* during five summers while earning degrees at the *University of Iowa*. After graduating, he joined this firm as a chemist in *Research & Development*. His professional career was interrupted by the *US Navy* serving as a hospital corpsman on the *Flagship of the Sixth Fleet, the USS Salem* (CA-139) operating in the Mediterranean Sea.

Upon his return to the States, he joined *Nalco Chemical Company* as a chemical sales engineer in *Nalco's Industrial Division*. He was promoted to field sales manager, and subsequently to *Nalco's International Division* as a corporate executive, working on four continents (North America, South America, Europe, and South Africa).

In South Africa, he facilitated the formation of a new specialty chemical company composed of *Nalco's Affiliate, African Explosives's Specialty Chemical Division*, and *Great Britain's ICI affiliate, Alfloc*.

He would leave Nalco, return to academia to pursue a **Ph.D.** in *Organizational, Industrial & Social Psychology*. Once earned, he consulted *Fortune 500* companies, *Contract Consultant* to **The American Management Association** (AMA), subsequently joining *Honeywell, Inc.* as a management & organizational development (OD) psychologist, eventually being promoted to *Honeywell International. SA* as director of human resources planning & development operating out of Brussels, Belgium.

Fisher has also been an adjunct professor at several colleges and universities including *The University of South Florida*, *St. Leo University*, *Florida Institute of Technology*, *Biscayne University*, *Nova University*, and *St. Petersburg College*.

To date, he has published 32 books and resides in Tampa, Florida with his wife, Betty. He can be reached by e-mail: thedeltagrpfl@cs.com or by checking his blog (peripateticphilosopher.blogspot.com).